THE CONSCIOUS PARENT'S
GUIDE TO

Childhood Anxiety

A mindful approach for helping
your child become calm, resilient,
and secure

Sherianna Boyle,
MEd, CAGS

Avon, Massachusetts

DEDICATION

*I dedicate this book to you, your children, and family. May your journey be
filled with love, possibility, growth, and inner strength.*

Published by
Adams Media, a division of F+W Media, Inc.
57 Littlefield Street, Avon, MA 02322. U.S.A.
www.adamsmedia.com

Contains material adapted from *The Everything® Parent's Guide to Overcoming Childhood
Anxiety* by Sherianna Boyle, MEd, CAGS, copyright © 2014 by F+W Media, Inc.,
ISBN 10: 1-4405-7706-4, ISBN 13: 978-1-4405-7706-2.

ISBN 10: 1-4405-9414-7
ISBN 13: 978-1-4405-9414-4
eISBN 10: 1-4405-9415-5
eISBN 13: 978-1-4405-9415-1

Printed in the United States of America.

10   9   8   7   6   5   4   3   2

This book is intended as general information only, and should not be used to diagnose or treat
any health condition. In light of the complex, individual, and specific nature of health problems,
this book is not intended to replace professional medical advice. The ideas, procedures, and suggestions in this book are intended to supplement, not replace, the advice of a trained medical
professional. Consult your physician before adopting any of the suggestions in this book, as well
as about any condition that may require diagnosis or medical attention. The author and publisher
disclaim any liability arising directly or indirectly from the use of this book.

Many of the designations used by manufacturers and sellers to distinguish their products are
claimed as trademarks. Where those designations appear in this book and F+W Media, Inc. was
aware of a trademark claim, the designations have been printed with initial capital letters.

Cover design by Alexandra Artiano.

*This book is available at quantity discounts for bulk purchases.
For information, please call 1-800-289-0963.*

Acknowledgments

This book opportunity arrived in the heat of summer. I want to thank my family for allowing me the time and space to write it. I also want to thank Adams Media for giving me the privilege to author this book. The subject matter couldn't be closer to what I choose to contribute to. To parents supporting their children through anxiety: I hear you, I commend you, and I truly honor your journey.

Contents

Introduction 11

CHAPTER 1: CONSCIOUS PARENTING. **13**
The Benefits of Conscious Parenting. 14
Giving Your Child Full Attention. 17
Understanding Behavior 18

CHAPTER 2: THE ANXIETY JOURNEY **21**
What's Happening for My Child? 22
Some Stress Is Good. 22
Worry Makes Anxiety Grow. 24
Your Child's Self-Awareness 29
The Stress and Anxiety Connection. 30
Is Anxiety Contagious? 32
Important Points to Consider. 33

CHAPTER 3: CAUSES OF ANXIETY **35**
How Common Is Anxiety? 36
Comparing Boys and Girls 36
Psychological Aspects 37
Biological Aspects 39
Genetic Causes 40
The Role of Temperament. 41
Environmental Factors 42
Important Points to Consider. 45

CHAPTER 4: SIGNS AND SYMPTOMS OF ANXIETY **47**
Behavioral Expressions 48
Avoidance 49
Feeling Isolated. 50
Skipping School 51

Homework Hassles. 53

Friendship Challenges 56

Body Talk. 57

Nervous Habits 59

Important Points to Consider. 59

CHAPTER 5: SCHOOL DAYS

CHAPTER 5: SCHOOL DAYS. **61**

Anxiety about School. 62

Expecting Anxiety 63

Test Anxiety. 63

Counter Negative Rehearsal 64

Handling Anxiety at School 66

Peers and Peer Pressure. 69

Bullies and Gossip 70

Middle-School Meltdowns 71

Staying Connected and Getting Involved .72

Important Points to Consider. 73

CHAPTER 6: OUTSIDE PRESSURES AND INFLUENCES

CHAPTER 6: OUTSIDE PRESSURES AND INFLUENCES **75**

Coping with Outside Pressures 76

Media. 77

Guidelines for Technology and Media 79

Social Media 82

Boundaries 83

Cyberbullying. 84

Other Influences. 85

Building Face-to-Face Social Skills 86

Important Points to Consider. 87

CHAPTER 7: BUILDING A SUPPORTIVE HOME ENVIRONMENT

CHAPTER 7: BUILDING A SUPPORTIVE HOME ENVIRONMENT **89**

Open Communication. 90

Reframing 93

Teaching Kids **How** to Feel. 94

It's a Family Affair. 95

Create a Support Team 95

Connect to Truth 96

Effects on Partnerships and Marriage 98

Parenting Style 99

Important Points to Consider. 100

CHAPTER 8: PARENTING AND ANXIETY..........................**101**

The Parent's Role...102

Seeing Choices as Tools...................................102

Thriving Parents Equal Thriving Children..................103

Overprotective Parenting 106

When Parents Are Depressed...............................108

How Is Your Marriage? 109

Separation, Divorce, and Blended Families 111

Important Points to Consider..............................113

CHAPTER 9: CONSCIOUS PARENTING POINTERS **115**

Consistency and Follow-Through 116

Being Active and Proactive................................118

Intentional Planning 118

Patience Really Is a Virtue................................119

Defuse Situations 121

Routine Is King..122

Co-Parenting..123

Transform Your Rules Into Empowerment Tools 125

Reframe Language 127

Strengthening Your Right Brain...........................128

Important Things to Consider 129

CHAPTER 10: DISCIPLINING CHILDREN WITH ANXIETY.............**131**

Self-Regulation over Self-Control 132

Using Logical and Natural Consequences 134

Logical Consequences 135

Natural Consequences....................................136

How Consequences Are Different from Punishment........137

Parenting Dos 138

Positive Reinforcement 139

Rewards 141

The Resilient Child......................................141

Important Points to Consider.............................142

CHAPTER 11: SELF-LOVE **145**

Liberating Anxiety 146

Breathing...147

Meditation..150

Progressive Muscle Relaxation 152
Creative Visualizations 153
Guided Imagery 154
Self-Talk. 155
From Worrywart to Worry Warrior 156
Self-Soothing Strategies. 157
Important Points to Consider. 162

CHAPTER 12: SELF-LOVE LIVING: EXERCISE, NUTRITION, AND SLEEP 163
Simple Ways to Curb Anxiety. 164
Foods That Can Increase Anxiety 166
Vitamins and Nutritional Supplements. 168
Exercise and Yoga. 171
Sleep Routine and Ritual. 172
Important Points to Consider. 176

CHAPTER 13: THE CASE FOR NATURAL HEALING: ALTERNATIVE THERAPIES 179
Massage 180
Acupuncture 182
Aromatherapy. 183
Biofeedback. 185
Energy Work. 187
Important Points to Consider. 188

CHAPTER 14: IF IT'S NOT ANXIETY, THEN WHAT?. 191
Overlap with ADD. 192
Overlap with Depression. 195
Adjustment Disorders 197
Developmental Transitions. 199
Shyness and Introversion 201
The Overextended Child. 203
Separation Anxiety. 204
Important Points to Consider. 205

CHAPTER 15: CHOOSING THERAPY 207
Individual, Family, and Group Therapy 208
Supportive Approaches 211

Play Therapy 213
Art and Music Therapy 214
Cognitive-Behavioral Therapy 215
When to Consider Medication. 217
Important Points to Consider. 217

CHAPTER 16: CREATING A PROMISING FUTURE **219**
What Is the Goal?. 220
Trust Yourself 223
Moving on from Medication. 226
Letting Go 227

Appendix: Additional Resources 231
Index 235

Introduction

What we have learned about the brain has dramatically changed over the past ten years. New scientific research has substantiated how vast, viable, and intricately connected our brains are. Yes, the number of diagnoses of anxiety in children and teens seems to be on the rise, but so are reliable and sound strategies proven to alleviate anxiety. Also increasing is the number of parents who are committed to conscious parenting. Rather than be paralyzed by their child's challenges, conscious parents choose to expose their children to life skills, tools, and strategies they may have never learned otherwise.

As a conscious parent, you can help your child use mind-body strategies and relaxation techniques to understand and work through the symptoms of anxiety. You can help your child learn that he has a choice in how he interprets and responds to the symptoms. If he feels overwhelmed or fearful of what can happen, he may select responses that do more harm than good. On the other hand, viewing his mind and body as a resource increases his ability to move through stress and fears with more confidence and ease.

Picking up a book on how to parent a child with anxiety may be the last thing you ever expected. No doubt it can feel a bit disheartening and uncomfortable. You may even experience a bit of your own fears and insecurities rising to the surface. But you've taken the first step in supporting your child through the symptoms of anxiety while building your child's inner resiliency.

The Conscious Parent's Guide to Childhood Anxiety recognizes anxiety as a journey of self-awareness, not just for your child, but for the entire family. Without this awareness, anxiety treatments and strategies may fall short, providing only short-term relief. As a result, your child's faith in his own abilities and progress may be compromised. Self-awareness takes knowledge, skills, and practice, but once acquired, your child will be one step closer to confidently taking control of his emotions and fears.

In the end, anxiety will no longer be something your child needs to beat, but rather an opportunity to strengthen his identity and character. Consider this book to be a doorway to revealing the true nature of your child.

Anxiety is not your child's identity, nor is it his future. It is an opportunity for your child to learn skills that allow him to become closer to who he *is*, rather than be stuck in who he isn't.

 **CHAPTER 1**

Conscious Parenting

Being a conscious parent is all about building strong, sustainable bonds with your children through mindful living and awareness. Traditional power-based parenting techniques that promote compliance and obedience can disconnect you from your children. Conscious parenting, on the other hand, helps you develop a positive emotional connection with your child. You acknowledge your child's unique self and attempt to empathize with his way of viewing the world. Through empathetic understanding and tolerance, you create a safe environment where your child feels his ideas and concerns are truly being heard. When you find yourself in a stressful situation with your child, rather than reacting with anger or sarcasm, conscious parenting reminds you to instead take a step back, reflect, and look for a peaceful solution—one that honors your child's individuality and motivations. This approach benefits all children, especially children with anxiety. You don't need to "fix" your child—you need to work with him to understand what triggers feelings of anxiety and how he can learn to overcome the symptoms. The strong bond built between you and your child, along with your own calm, respectful attitude, help him to feel calm, confident, and secure.

The Benefits of Conscious Parenting

Conscious parenting isn't a set of rules or regulations that you must follow; rather, it is a system of beliefs. Conscious parents engage and connect with their children, using mindful and positive discipline rather than punishment. They try to be present when they're spending time with their children, avoiding distractions like TV and social media. Conscious parents respect their children and accept them as they are. The most important part of conscious parenting is building an emotional connection with your child so you can understand the underlying reasons for behavior.

Conscious parenting is about listening with full attention, and embracing an acceptance of yourself and your child without judgment. As you engage in the act of *becoming*, you will discover a heightened sense of emotional awareness of yourself and your child, a clearer self-regulation in the parenting relationship, and a greater compassion for yourself and your child.

Conscious parenting brings with it a number of benefits including improved communication, stronger relationships, and the feeling of greater happiness and satisfaction in life. Some of these benefits appear more immediately, while others take some time to emerge. The benefits of conscious parenting and mindfulness are a result of making it a part of your daily life. With practice, conscious parenting becomes an integral part of who and how you are in the world, and will in turn become a central part of who your child is, as well.

SELF-AWARENESS AND SELF-CONTROL

One of the first benefits of conscious parenting that you (and your child) will see is a heightened awareness of yourself and your inner life, including your emotions, thoughts, and feelings. As you become more aware of these various forces moving within you, you can begin to watch them rise without being at their mercy. For example, when you are aware that you are becoming angry, you have a choice about whether to act from that anger or attend to that feeling directly. You will start to notice the things that tend to set you off, your triggers, and you will begin to be able to anticipate your emotions before they have a hold on you.

Mindfulness is the practice of being attentive in every moment, and noticing what is taking place both inside and outside of you without judgment. It is the practice of purposefully seeing your thoughts, emotions, experiences, and surroundings as they arise. Simply put, mindfulness is the act of paying attention.

As you become more skilled at noticing the thoughts and feelings that arise, you will begin to notice them more quickly, maybe even before they start to affect your actions. This awareness is itself a powerful tool. It opens up the possibility to say, "Hey, I'm pretty mad right now" instead of yelling at somebody you care about because you were upset about something else. It can do exactly the same thing for your child, helping her to learn to communicate about her feelings rather than just react from that place of emotion. As with most things, children learn this best by seeing it modeled by the adults in their lives.

Often, you may notice that your emotions carry with them a sense of urgency. This mindfulness creates a certain amount of mental space in which you can deal with the thought or feeling itself rather than being moved to act by it. As you feel the impulse to do something arise within you, you will be able to identify the forces driving that sense of "I need to do something." They could be, for example, the thoughts that come up as you watch a three-year-old put on her own shoes. Your mind might be buzzing with impatience, and the thought "I need to put her shoes on for her because she's taking forever" may arise. When you notice this thought, you'll have some room to check in with yourself and act intentionally instead of just reacting or immediately acting on it.

WELL-BEING

Conscious parents understand that all they do and say over the course of each day *matters*. It is a sense of the *now*, being in the present moment without regard or worry for the past or future. When you become more mindful, you may find that you become more accepting of the things in life that you can't change and experience less stress. The net result is greater satisfaction and enjoyment of whatever each day has to offer. This sense of well-being offers a satisfaction and contentment in knowing that we are who we are intended to be, doing precisely what we are designed for in the moment.

As human beings, we each possess the tools for contributing something of value. Assess your gifts and talents—those personality traits and skills that make you unique—and determine how to employ them to enhance your parenting. If you take a full accounting of yourself—good, bad, and indifferent—and *own* the sum total of your individual experience, you are taking the first step toward conscious parenting.

EMPATHY

The awareness you gain as a conscious parent has the practical purpose of redefining your perception of yourself and your compassionate understanding of your child. When you understand how your child experiences the world and how she learns, you can communicate in ways that really reach her. This largely happens through modeling, or teaching through example. Doing so allows you to pass on the values and lessons that are important to you, regardless of your beliefs.

What do you believe about stress? What do you think a life without anxiety looks like? If you believe stress is a burden or that stress is the reason for your child's problems, this will influence how you approach your child's symptoms. If you believe that life without anxiety means a perfect world without stress, your relationship with stress may be based more on frustration than confidence. It turns out that what you believe about stress matters. Your beliefs create mindsets, and mindsets influence the way you view your child's symptoms. Part of supporting your child through anxiety is to become informed about stress (and anxiety) and when to be concerned, as well as how it may be utilized to her advantage.

ACCEPTANCE AND VALIDATION

Your child relies upon you and your family to provide a solid foundation of self-esteem. Equipped with a strong sense of self-worth, your child will be better prepared to enter into a life that will likely present many challenges. Much of your time and energy will be expended in raising, counseling, and disciplining your child in ways that she will understand. Try to equalize those occasions by reinforcing your love and appreciation of her gifts and talents.

Giving Your Child Full Attention

All too often people multitask their way through the day. This is a coping mechanism you have probably developed as a means of juggling the many projects, tasks, errands, and obligations that you are responsible for. Although it is a common approach to managing the multiple things you have to do, it splits your attention in ways that distract your mind and actually lessen the quality of your attention. In reality, heavy multitasking causes your work and social interactions to suffer because of how it divides your focus.

To avoid this becoming an issue between you and your child (and to make sure you're modeling the kind of focus and engagement you want your child to use as well), make sure to practice engaged listening when you are at home with your family. This means setting aside other distractions, making eye contact, and giving the speaker (in this case, your child) your full attention.

Even if you set down what you are doing and are looking at your child, check in with yourself. Is your mind focused on what he is saying, or is it still planning, scheduling, remembering, projecting, or worrying? It is very easy to only half-listen, and this can be especially true when it comes to listening to children.

True multitasking is neurologically impossible. When you try to multitask, what you actually end up doing is rapidly switching between tasks. Each time you do so, you lose efficiency and concentration, so stop trying! Do one thing at a time so you can do it with your whole brain, then move on to the next.

The stories your child tells are not always relevant or very interesting to your adult life. The idea behind active listening is not that you suddenly care about what everyone else brought to school for Show and Tell today, it's that you care about your child, and he wants to tell you the funny, strange, or interesting things that he experienced that day. The important part of this interaction is that your child wants to share his joy, curiosity, and interests with you. He wants to interact with you and share parts of himself and his life with you, and this is one of the ways he can do that. Be open to this gift. You'll be surprised by the interest you may develop in these things as you listen to your child talk. When a person you love cares about something, it becomes easier to see that thing through his eyes and appreciate it all the more.

Understanding Behavior

Anxiety can be triggered by a myriad of things. Thoughts trigger anxiety, particularly ones that focus on flaws or unworthiness. Emotions such as shame and guilt are anxiety magnifiers, along with worry, learning difficulties, pressure, uncertainty, feeling emotionally unsafe, and fear of criticism and/or failure. Unrealistic expectations, striving for perfection, and an imagined sense of doom also contribute to this state. Long-term anxiety leads to a habit of racing thoughts and a persistent desire for things to be a certain way, or different from the way they are at that moment. Finally, anxiety may be triggered by the memory of past events, both those that are within the child's current awareness as well as some that may be buried in her subconscious mind.

Anxiety can also be triggered by development. Children go through several stages of anxiety as they grow, and their brain develops and readjusts to newly acquired knowledge. For example, an infant of a certain age can experience anxiety when a parent or caregiver leaves a room. The infant believes the parent has ceased to exist, when in reality the parent may just be in the next room. This is a type of separation anxiety, which can occur from around eight months old through the preschool years, and it is normal for a child of this age to show intense feelings if separated from her parents.

At two years old, your child may be scared of the dark, loud noises, animals, changes in the house, or strangers. At age five you can add "bad people" and fear of bodily harm to the list. By age six, it is common for children to still be afraid of the dark and have separation issues again, as well as fear of thunder and lightning, supernatural beings, staying alone, or getting hurt. Within the age range of seven to eight, it is common for children to unconsciously bite their pencils or twirl their hair as a temporary way to relieve tension.

Kids aged seven through twelve often have fears that are more reality-based, like getting hurt or of some kind of disaster happening, because they are now more aware of the world around them. Teens may show signs of fear of the future, failure, rejection, or disappointment.

All these fears are developmentally normal phases, but if your child seems stuck in a phase or fixated on a certain fear it may be a sign of something more. Many children can be described as intensely oversensitive, or "high maintenance," which may just be a normal expression of your child's developing personality. The deciding factors of whether to seek help lie in the *frequency* and *intensity* of the fears, and *how much* the fear and worry interferes with life.

CHAPTER 2

The Anxiety Journey

Kids today face great academic, social, and emotional challenges. These challenges and pressures cause some of them to experience anxiety. They are unable to be at ease and enjoy the moment. Instead they find themselves locked up in their thoughts, buried by fears, and drawn toward distractions. Quick-fix approaches such as lecturing, avoiding certain situations, or constantly reassuring them are slowly losing their promise. These ideas are gradually being replaced by a shift of insight focusing less on what is wrong with a child and more on how symptoms work and what is causing them. As you work with your child to understand anxiety, you will learn what emotions are made of. The most important part of this process is to shift from trying to understand what is happening *to* your child, to becoming curious about how this may be happening *for* him.

What's Happening for My Child?

Learning about anxiety can help both you *and* your child. Your child will have an opportunity to learn about the magnificence of his brain, body, and feelings. He will learn how thoughts manifest into words, self-talk, and, in some cases, belief systems. He will also learn the difference between suffering and feeling.

"Mindfulness means paying attention to things as they actually are in any given moment, however they are, rather than as we want them to be." —Jon Kabat-Zinn

Through feeling, he will connect to the deeper parts of himself, and because you are along for the ride you get to join him in discovering your inner values, how you interpret the world, what triggers uncomfortable feelings for you, and your own unconscious and conscious fears and desires. With your guidance, rather than becoming overwhelmed by his symptoms, your child will learn how to appreciate them, and with practice use them to make healthier choices. The process of overcoming anxiety takes your child along a journey of creating healthy boundaries, developing resiliency, self-discipline, creativity, autonomy, and most of all self-love. As his parent, you are an important guide and supporter.

Some Stress Is Good

Research indicates a *low* amount of stress does no damage to the body and can actually be good for you, as it helps you to tackle tasks and complete your to-do lists. Author and Stanford psychologist Kelly McGonigal, PhD, is pioneering some of the latest research, highlighting much of it in her book *The Upside of Stress*, including the idea that "stress can in fact make us stronger, smarter, and happier if we learn how to embrace it." If your child didn't have *some* stress in her life, she might be less motivated to study for exams, complete homework assignments, or excel in music or sports.

On the other hand, when stress runs at high levels, instead of being motivated your child may become paralyzed by what she is experiencing. This can lead to an increase of symptoms such as self-doubt, chronic worrying, insecurity, fear of the future, and a tendency to hang on to the past. Your child may experience symptoms like stomach irritability, tension headaches, difficulty sleeping, nervousness, distractibility, irritability, and anger. She may find it difficult to try new things or make friends.

COPING

A child who is feeling anxious may find her own way of coping with what she is feeling. Without a true understanding of anxiety and guidance for how to move through the symptoms, this could lead to counterproductive habits and behaviors. For example, she may try to distract herself by fiddling with her phone or avoiding certain situations altogether. She may watch several hours of television to avoid studying for a test. Some children turn to overeating for comfort. A younger child might become clingy or have bouts of tantrums. As a caregiver, you can help your child learn healthy and more effective coping strategies to deal with anxiety. For example:

- Break down tasks, like homework, household chores, or musical instrument practice into manageable chunks.

- Expose your child to a new situation ahead of time. Visit a new school, ask a coach about what's needed for a first practice, or do some online research on a new activity.

- Teach your child to plan ahead. Ask your child to think about what she needs to go school, to the pool, or to a game. Try not to list things for her—ask her to come up with a list on her own.

- Losing things can be anxiety provoking. Help your child come up with a strategy for keeping track of her belongings. Encourage her to think for herself and be responsible for remembering to bring items home.

In general, the best coping strategies are those that put your child in control of her environment. While you may want to protect her from the distressing feelings of anxiety, make sure you're not constantly "protecting" your child from situations that can cause stress. Allowing your child to avoid school events, birthday parties, and play dates will not make the anxiety go away. Your child needs to learn to identify stressful situations and come up with her own ways to deal with them (with your help, of course).

Worry Makes Anxiety Grow

Everyone worries. On the positive side, worry can motivate you to do well at a task, accomplish a goal, or take care of a problem. With mental discipline and patience, your child will be able to reflect back on his experiences as opportunities rather than obstacles. He will eventually realize there are no monsters hiding in the closet; that if he makes a mistake, he will live through it; and sometimes he has to keep trying to get what he wants. However, for some children, anxiety is so overwhelming that it becomes paralyzing and prevents any movement whatsoever. Worries become a full-time job.

As a parent, you may also unconsciously be adding to your child's worries. Some parents get in the habit of hearing about a child's worry and sending (silently or verbally) one of their own worries back to the child. For example, a child who expresses disappointment or worry about school may trigger a parent's fear of "what if this school or teacher doesn't work out, how will I handle it?" A parent may also begin to believe that this is a sign that this will be a "bad" year. Before you add to your child's worries, take a minute to close your eyes and pay attention to your own feelings. Place your hand on your lower abdomen and on inhale press your belly away from your spine (like you were blowing up a balloon) and on exhale gently tug your abdomen toward your spine. Breathing in this way sends a calming sensation that can be contagious. Just as children can sense when you are in a state of fear or tension they can also sense calm and serenity. Breathing in this way increases the opportunity for you to experience emotions such as love and trust. Directing your attention to your child in this state is no different than sending him vibrations of confidence and peace.

WHEN THE "WHAT IFS" KICK IN

Worry involves both thoughts and feelings, and is defined as a lasting preoccupation with past or future events. This type of thinking causes your child to feel as if he were reliving an event repeatedly, or constantly readying himself for the worst outcome in a future event. When you see your child "becoming his anxiety," meaning he sees himself as having nervousness, worry, or lacking control rather than experiencing it, you might think to yourself, "I don't get it, where did this come from?" There is a huge difference between "having" and experiencing. To have anxiety is no different than saying, "I am anxiety" whereas to experience anxiety is like saying, "I am experiencing worry, doubt, and fear." It is important to teach children that their experiences do not define them or their future. Instead, focus on the present moment where the body, breath, and mind are always growing and changing.

As a parent the worry will often seem out of proportion to you and sometimes seem as if it came out of nowhere. You see your child get stuck in a vicious cycle that in turn increases his dread, and nothing you say or do seems to help. When your child is trapped by worry, you will often hear the phrases "if only . . ." and "what if . . ." over and over.

THE "WHAT IFS"

"What if" refers to thoughts about the future. In the case of worry, these thoughts are about any number of emotionally charged things that could possibly happen. *What if I am not liked by the other kids, do not do well on the test, cannot hit the ball in gym,* or *do not get chosen for the team? What if my face turns red during my speech,* or *my teacher gets upset that I forgot my homework again?* When the worry starts and your child cannot stop it, it grows in intensity like a runaway train, and your child ultimately ends up wondering, *What if no matter what I do, it is not enough?* It is an endless cycle that can never be resolved and often results in negative self-talk, low self-esteem, and ultimately, being unsure of who he is. It also shows itself behaviorally. When *what if* takes hold over your child's life, he may seem paralyzed, unable to participate in activities or unable to perform to his capability. You then will hear phrases like, "What if I don't catch the ball when it comes my way? I can't be on the team," or "I can't try out for the play. What if I forget my lines? Everyone will make fun of me—I'll just die."

REDIRECTING WHAT IFS

There are two ways to handle *what if*. The first is to focus on the moment by redirecting your awareness to your body. Parents can model this by saying, "I notice that when I think about *what if*, my jaw tightens and my shoulders tense up. My eyes grow wide, and I stop noticing what is around me." Dr. Lawrence J. Cohen, author of *The Opposite of Worry*, suggests you teach children to change their thoughts from *what if* to *what is*. This can be encouraged by directing your child to his own body as a resource for restoring balance. Initially, children may be fearful of noticing what is happening physically; however, when practiced in a gentle, nonjudgmental way, noticing transforms into expanding awareness and observation of the situation. Go ahead and try it on yourself. Notice if one of your shoulders feels tight, and watch how your body naturally begins to relax itself simply as a result of that noticing.

The second way is to reframe *what if* to *I look forward to*. For example, your child may say, "What if my face turns red while I give my speech?" Teach him to reframe this and say, "I look forward to getting through this speech." *Reframing* teaches children how to shift present thinking from the negative to the positive. This shift functions on a neurological level; because negative thinking increases stress hormones, giving your child's body the impression that what he is thinking is actually happening, reframing it in a positive way reduces those stress hormones, allowing the body to relax.

Your body does not know the difference between a real or imagined threat. If you imagine yourself having a conflict with someone, your body will respond as if it is in danger. Most likely your breathing will become shallow and rapid; you may feel tense, irritated, or even angry. Your body does not know you are imagining this through your thoughts and images; it reacts as if the threat is genuine.

THE "IF ONLYS"

If only refers to thoughts about an unhappy event that your child wishes had not happened. Maybe your child said something to a friend he now wishes he had not, or did something he regrets. The event has ultimately left him with an unresolved emotional feeling, and worry is how his mind tries to resolve it, by trying to figure out what went wrong and how to fix it. *If only* statements sound like this: *If only I had kept my mouth shut when Sara asked me what I thought of her new haircut; now she will never talk to me again*, or *If only I had listened in class, I would have gotten a better grade on this test*.

If your child is stuck in the past and unable to escape memories of a negative experience, you can teach him releasing strategies to allow him to move forward and leave the memory in the past.

In many cases, the event has already happened and your child cannot control the past, nothing can be done to alter it, and worry cycles on without resolution like a gerbil on an exercise wheel. Your child can become consumed with guilt, hypersensitive to criticism, and hesitant to take action for fear of yet another "failure." However, you can use your knowledge of your child's worry cycle to teach him how his brain works, how he has the ability to influence the activity of his brain cells, and in what way his neurotransmitters fire and wire. In order to do so, your child will need to follow these three basic steps:

1. Notice his thoughts
2. Observe his thoughts without judgment
3. Experience his thoughts through breathing and bodily sensation

Thoughts can be either conscious or unconscious. In the purest form, each thought is a unit of energy that gives off an electromagnetic frequency. These frequencies are the building blocks of emotions. High-frequency emotions are ones that lift you up, like joy, love, and appreciation. Low-frequency emotions, such as guilt and shame, weigh you down, often coloring your perception with negativity and doubt.

Your child's thoughts and feelings are a form of energetic vibration. For example, if you think about something you are fearful of your body will tense up. This is an indication that your energy on the inside has become slow, sluggish, or dense. It is almost as if your energy is momentarily in a traffic jam. As you bring your attention to your body (for example, drop your awareness on your lower belly), notice how this activates the breath. It is your breath and body that allow the movement of fear. In other words, the traffic jam begins to open up. As a result you and your child feel better, more capable, and hopeful.

As your child becomes more skilled in self-observation he will learn he can experience feelings without labeling or creating a story around them. Habitual thoughts tend to get memorized and therefore familiar. This means the same neurochemicals get programmed in the same routine way. As your child begins to change, his neurochemicals will fire in a new way. Like most things your child attempts for the first time, this approach may initially feel a bit uncomfortable or uncertain. See this discomfort as a sign of growth. Thoughts spark feelings, and as your child learns the relationship between thoughts and feelings, he will soon recognize his own ability to influence the way he feels.

No doubt a hug, pat on the back, or words of appreciation can go a long way. However, keep in mind that some parents can go overboard in helping a child "feel" better. Conscious parents provide guidance and support without needing to control the child's experiences.

According to Joe Dispenza, author of *Evolve Your Brain: The Science of Changing Your Mind* and *Breaking the Habit of Being Yourself*, "Thoughts are the language of the brain and feelings are the language of the body." The body is always in the present moment (where anxiety cannot live). For example, imagine you are studying with your child and he says, "I don't know the answer." Rather than tell your child the answer, you could suggest that he pause, and sit with the problem a minute before saying "I don't know." Very often a child has the answer but he has developed a rote response as a way to push through uncomfortable feelings. Once he sits and lets the question rest in his body rather than push it through with his thoughts, he may discover he knew more than he initially thought.

Your Child's Self-Awareness

Rather than focus on a child's self-esteem, conscious parents place more attention on self-awareness. To be self-aware means to notice your thoughts, beliefs, and feelings without judgment. Self-esteem comes from whether or not your child sees herself as a basically good, worthy, and competent person, despite the fact that she may on occasion experience negative emotions like sadness, frustration, and fear. The key is to become aware of these emotions and thoughts without identifying with them. As your child develops this skill, she will be empowered by her ability to move through these experiences rather than be overwhelmed by them.

PERFECTION

Your child may place too much emphasis on "perfection." She may be unable to appreciate what she does well, or upset about her limitations. This type of mindset makes mistakes appear bigger, creating a negative outlook full of personal criticism. The negativity may translate to seeing herself as incompetent, inadequate, or imperfect, and it can also lead to a rigid, inflexible view of people and life. The types of statements you might hear are *How could I have missed that, I'm so stupid*, or *I didn't get invited . . . nobody likes me.*

Often, if what your child did accomplish is not 100 percent a success, she considers herself a failure. This thinking becomes a crippling and painful way to live, and restricts your child's opportunities to be human and learn from her mistakes.

Most of us grew up with the mindset that practice makes perfect. Author Jim Kwik from Kwik Learning (*www.jimkwik.com*) teaches kids *practice makes permanent*. This means what you choose to do over and over again is what you will remember. If self-criticism is something you do on a regular basis, those negative critical statements become imprinted into the subconscious mind. The good news is that you can reprogram your brain simply by mindfully changing your negative thoughts and self-statements to positive ones.

When your child focuses more on being present in the moment and less on the final outcome, she is less likely to feel the pressures of perfectionism. Consciously moving through anxiety means your child will focus less on *doing* and more on *being*.

The Stress and Anxiety Connection

Stress can come from any situation or thought that causes your child to feel frustrated, angry, nervous, or tense. What is stressful to one child will not necessarily be stressful to another. Stress is subjective, and often parents do not experience stress the same way their children do. Parents also do not feel stress about the same *things* as their children do. Understanding what is stressful for your child and responding, even if the issue seems trivial, will help your child build his overall sense of security.

For example, if your child tells you he is afraid of the dark and wants to sleep with a light on, it will not be helpful to say, "Oh, that's silly; there is nothing out there. I already checked." The child who tends to feel stress or anxiety will believe that you do not know what you are talking about, he might feel confused about whether to trust you or himself, and his symptoms may grow.

Stress can lead to depression, eating disorders, or a host of other difficulties. The impact is usually cumulative, adding up over time, and sometimes culminating in an anxiety disorder. Consider each time your child experiences stress and anxiety as an opportunity to interrupt the cycle and redirect your child's sense of security, self, and competence. Becoming aware of what seems stressful in your child's life gives you the power to intervene and reroute the cycle. Here are some of the emotional or behavioral signs of a stressed child:

- Worry
- Inability to relax
- Irritability
- Chronic fatigue
- Over- or undereating
- Critical of self and others
- Overly sensitive
- New or recurring fears (fear of the dark, being alone, of strangers)
- Clinging or unwilling to let go of Mom or Dad
- Unexplained anger
- Unwarranted crying
- Aggressive or refusal behavior
- Regression to a behavior that is typical of an earlier developmental stage (like bedwetting or thumb sucking)
- Unwillingness to participate in family or school activities
- Shyness that limits activities
- Headaches
- Upset stomach
- Sleep disturbances
- Stuttering

Teach your child how to divert his stress-triggered anxiety before it leads to something more intense such as an illness, conflict in relationships, or a negative impact on schoolwork.

Is Anxiety Contagious?

Have you ever spent time with someone who was anxious? You probably sensed tension or irritability. Before you knew it, you might have found your own mood changing or your heart rate elevating in response. If you are around someone who is complaining, critical, or negative, you could easily get swept up into his state of mind if you are not aware enough to consciously choose to reject it. However, by remaining in the moment and being aware of your own body, you create an inner resiliency, making you less susceptible to the anxiety of others, and you are more likely to make choices that support your personal self-confidence and mental and emotional health.

SELF-REFLECTION

It is common for your child to be stressed if she sees that you are stressed. For the sake of your child, you may need to learn to reduce your stress by reflecting on it without judgment. Reflection without judgment occurs when the mind and body are in harmony with one another, which reduces anxiety. To achieve this balance, follow these steps.

First, open the doorway to nonjudgment by choosing to connect to your heart. Sit quietly, close your eyes, and allow yourself to feel the present moment. Imagine the sun is shining on your face, heart, and body. Next, take a deep breath. Notice how this opens you up to receiving rather than resisting what is happening in and around you.

After two or three receiving breaths, ask yourself:

O Am I overbooked or overwhelmed?

O Am I worried or having trouble sleeping?

O Am I forgetting to eat well, exercise, or take time for myself?

○ Do I allow myself to hear my child's concerns, or do I put my hand in the air and say things like, "I have had enough" or "I can't handle this"?

Once you are able to understand your emotions and what stresses you, you will feel calmer and better able to help your child. You can be a powerful model and example of healthy stress management and self-care for your child. Be the best person you can be for her sake, as well as yours.

Important Points to Consider

You are your child's best teacher, and that holds true in many situations, especially when learning to deal with her anxiety. Listen to your child's concerns, model good self-awareness when you feel stress yourself, and most importantly, keep an open line of communication with your child. One of the best ways to reduce your child's stress is to be there for her when anxiety creeps up upon her. As a conscious parent you know that open communication and connecting with your child is vital to reducing her anxiety. As you and your child explore anxiety, keep these points in mind:

○ Learning about how anxiety works can have benefits for both you and your child. Understanding how your child experiences symptoms will help you to empathize.

○ Realize that stress is inevitable in life, and some stress is actually beneficial.

○ As you help your child to become more self-aware, you're helping her to recognize negative thoughts and emotions without identifying with them.

○ Be aware that your anxiety is noticeable to your child. Take the time to show your child that you are able to manage stress and calm yourself when you're stressed.

 **CHAPTER 3**

Causes of Anxiety

As a conscious parent, you need to know what your child is going through so you can empathize with her feelings and emotions. With that in mind, prepare yourself by understanding the causes and characteristics of anxiety so you can be ready for any questions or concerns your child may have. Anxiety occurs for a variety of emotional, biological, and environmental reasons. It is built on factors that are interrelated, including genetics, temperament, brain chemistry, home environment, trauma, and stress. Learning about the underlying causes of your child's individual anxiety will help you to understand what she is experiencing. Focusing on the causes of behavior, rather than the behavior itself, will help you to empathize with your child so you can work together to overcome anxiety.

How Common Is Anxiety?

With over 40 million adults diagnosed worldwide, anxiety has become the most widely recognized mental health problem in the general population. According to the Anxiety and Depression Association of America (ADAA), anxiety disorders affect one in eight children. If left untreated or avoided, children with anxiety disorders are at a higher risk to perform poorly in school, miss out on important social experiences, and engage in substance abuse.

Fear-based messages embedded into culture and magnified through media using visual imaging, sounds, and words stimulate stress while creating and feeding a global anxiety. Marketers often use this to their advantage, pushing quick-fix strategies via a tone of needing more, being unsafe, or being inadequate. In many ways this has led to a desensitization of immoral acts, and to the suppression of the two inherent qualities that give human beings the ability to alleviate anxiety: empathy and compassion. Fortunately, the tools and strategies in this book support the growth and development of those powerful emotions.

Comparing Boys and Girls

Although there is no clear-cut reason, researchers do recognize some differences between boys and girls. Medical professionals suggest that girls are perhaps more likely to have a hormonal imbalance, an increased level of emotional, mental, and physical changes, and a higher sensitivity to others' struggles. A study led by Tara M. Chaplin of the Department of Psychiatry at Yale University School of Medicine found that boys and girls have very different emotional tendencies. Her study of over 21,000 participants found that in infancy, the boys and girls exhibited similar emotional displays. As the children aged and were introduced to social settings, they felt the need to conform to social norms, which may have led to a sense that they could not freely express their true emotions. Adolescent girls demonstrated higher levels of shame and guilt, while boys were more likely to exhibit anger and aggression. Researcher Carol Gilligan, when comparing girls and boys, discovered that girls perceive danger in their isolation, with abandonment being a main fear, whereas boys described danger as more entrapment or smothering.

Your child's perceptions are influenced by her bodily sensations. Strategies such as breathing increase your child's bodily sensations. As this occurs, her emotions are able to move more freely. This in turn helps her to feel more capable and confident. Teach your child about sensations. For example, when you breathe mindfully (tuning in to the moment) while noticing your body you are likely to feel sensations such as tingly, warm, or even a bit floaty. This experience is your body's way of not only releasing stress but also rewiring itself for centeredness. Individuals who learn how to breathe mindfully often report feeling better, more focused, capable, and clear.

While it may be true that girls and boys tend to behave differently, try not to generalize when talking about your child. It may seem harmless to talk about boys being more active and girls being more emotional, but this can negatively influence behavior and learning. Parents should watch how stereotypes are reinforced in their speech used at home; phrases such as "boys will be boys" or "girls are so dramatic" can teach children to disguise their feelings and to behave in ways that they perceive as predetermined or expected by society.

Scientists also believe sex hormones may play a role in anxiety for both boys and girls. During times of intense hormonal shifts, symptoms of anxiety may occur. In some cases, it could also be the anxiety that exacerbates the intensity of the hormonal shift. In general, girls are more likely than boys to seek help. This may reflect the fact that it is more socially acceptable for girls to both express and address their emotional states.

Psychological Aspects

Your child learns primarily by imitation. Studies have found that 95 percent of children's learning occurs unconsciously and is influenced by how children interpret what they see. Keep in mind you are being watched and your decisions and responses are being used to make judgments about what life looks and feels like to your child. Remember that a child's or adolescent's brain will view things differently than the adult brain.

FEELINGS IN THE FAMILY

Growing up in a family where fear, worry, and anxiety are consistently modeled by parents or family members may teach a child to be anxious. In addition, if a child grows up in a home where a parent or sibling is terminally ill, in an abusive or alcoholic home where she is walking on eggshells around a parent, or constantly in an over-alert state, she may learn to expect the worst, or actually *look* for the worst. The child ends up living in a state of constant worry.

The psychological state of fear and trauma can also be present when a child is bullied at school, in the neighborhood, or on the school bus. The continuous state of anxiety that results creates children who might freeze up or withdraw in order to protect themselves. They have a tendency to lose their sense of belonging and separate themselves from friends. A typical example is the child who is standing off on his own during lunch or recess. It is also common for a child feeling anxiety to fall into a world of his own where he might feel he has to create plans for how to safeguard himself, "just in case." When this happens, the body and mind's resources are sidetracked, and your child's growth may become interrupted.

INTERNAL VERSUS EXTERNAL STRESSORS

The term *internal* refers to the vulnerability that comes from genetics and temperament. It also means how your child feels inside about what happens externally or around her. Internal triggers are more likely to affect a child who has strong emotions or who has a tendency to be a sensitive child. Examples of internal cues that can lead to anxiety are guilt, anger, shame, perfectionism, negative thinking, and frequent thoughts that are centered on *should*, *must*, and *never*.

External influences are events that happen outside of the child and have a separate point of origin. Examples of some external triggers are divorce, violence at home, school, games or TV, injury, illness or death of a family member, abuse, or a disaster.

The amount of anxiety your child feels from these triggers will be based on how she processes it. Therefore, it will be important for you to take the time to help your child separate out what is a real threat external to her from what she is creating internally, through her own thoughts.

Biological Aspects

Fear and panic are normal reactions to danger. When fear or panic is felt, this reflects a chain of events in your child's autonomic nervous system. By learning to understand how your child's body works, you can then explain it to your child. Children who understand how their body is working *for* them rather than *against* them tend to be less overwhelmed by the emotional shifts they feel inside. Explain to your child how every thought secretes a chemical, which creates a feeling. If you think fearful thoughts, your body cooperates by delivering fearful emotions. On the contrary, if you think loving thoughts, like how much you love your pet, your body delivers those emotions.

Teach your child that just because he thinks something that doesn't mean it's true. For example, a child may think that no one likes him. But this doesn't mean it's true. It's normal to have a variety of thoughts, but when your child chooses to believe his negative thoughts, this can lead to stress and anxiety.

NEUROTRANSMITTERS

A person's brain is a network of billions of nerve cells called neurons that communicate with each other to create thoughts, emotions, and behaviors. This process is called cell-to-cell communication, in which a transfer of information from one part of the brain to another is made possible by chemicals called neurotransmitters. The two primary neurotransmitters that affect your child's feelings are serotonin and dopamine.

THE AMYGDALA AND HIPPOCAMPUS

When the fight-or-flight response is triggered it occurs in the parts of the brain called the amygdala and hippocampus. The amygdala is the part of the brain where feelings and emotions are based. So if your child is feeling fearful and anxious, the amygdala will send this information throughout your child's body in an alert. The hippocampus holds memory, time, and place, especially for situations that are highly emotional. Once the amygdala jumps into action, your child can become overly sensitive to certain stimuli. It may seem like your child is consumed with worry at the moment; however, it is likely your child is revisiting the emotion of worry from the past, meaning that at some point in his life he might have experienced worry and this has been stored away in the brain and body. Parents who spend time analyzing and evaluating past events to look for clues for how worry may have surfaced are likely to enter the worry cycle themselves. You are better off putting your time and attention into the present moment that is you and your child's body and breath. Over time old reactions (worries) will begin to loosen while new responses are created. For example, your child might be nervous about speaking up in public. His heart may start to beat faster and he becomes nervous, sweaty, and insecure. Initially you may react by reassuring him, but he continues to panic. Consider instead the public speaking is bringing to light nervousness which already existed, meaning that the fear did not cause the nervousness— it revealed it.

Children are more likely to remember things that have an emotional charge. Parents can help reinforce positive memories by keeping them alive through pictures, videos, and storytelling.

Genetic Causes

Investigations into the causes of anxiety are clear that anxiety, panic, and depression can be hereditary, and that anxiety is usually a concern for several members of the same family. If a parent or sibling has a history of anxiety or depression, a child's risk increases four- to six-fold for developing symptoms herself. This is because the structure of the brain and its processes are inherited. However, solid evidence is emerging that not only can you change your brain but also your DNA (genetic makeup). Studies on consciousness and awareness now prove human beings can actually influence what gets passed on to future generations. Families with patterns of anxiety can now take comfort in the knowledge that the cycle of unnecessary worry can truly be broken. People who have no family history of the disorder can develop anxiety as well. Knowing your family history helps you and any professionals supporting you make clear, conscious decisions about what steps to take.

The Role of Temperament

Temperament is your child's nature present at birth. Many parents can tell almost immediately whether their child will be peaceful, irritable, sociable, or more introverted. At the forefront of temperament research is Dr. Jerome Kagan of Harvard University, now retired. What he discovered in timid children is that the amygdala is more easily aroused in those prone to fearfulness, creating children who are more anxious and uneasy. Compared to children in the other groups, their hearts beat faster when confronted with stressful situations, they were more finicky about eating, were introverted around strangers, and were reluctant to try anything new. Kagan found that from birth, these children had a hyperexcitable right temporal lobe in their brains, and if fear was triggered in the child, those pathways became stronger. More research is needed, but other studies have shown that the hippocampus is smaller in people who have had a significant trauma.

The brain is constantly changing. It will reforge neural pathways and connections based on information it receives, changing itself in order to learn and respond. It is a work in progress and becomes stronger through repetition and time. Parents who are more successful in reducing their child's fearfulness and anxiety will allow the child to face fears and work through them so the preferred pathways can become stronger. It is best to challenge your child in small increments, no matter how uncomfortable, while being encouraging and loving. The good news is that temperament and personality are not fixed. They can and will be altered to your child's benefit as he learns to integrate coping and release strategies into his daily life.

Environmental Factors

The environment is composed of all events, people, circumstances, desires, needs, and situations that have a point of origin outside of your child. Any situation that disrupts your child's sense of structure and order in his world creates a change internally.

LIFE EVENTS

It is common when children start school or daycare, or transition to a new grade, for them to become emotional, scared, or clingy for a brief period. Usually, parents will find a few weeks are normal for the transition, and are able to hang in there. It is when the reaction becomes protracted and your child cannot move past his feelings about the incident that intervention will be necessary. Some common examples of stressful life events (which are external stressors) are:

- A trauma
- Seeing violence at home, school, or on TV
- School issues
- Divorce
- Moving
- Loss
- Anxious, overprotective, or critical parenting style
- Difficulty with friendships
- Death of a family member, friend, or family pet

UNCERTAINTY

When a situation lacks a clear outcome, your child might feel a lack of control and significant stress. Uncertain as to what type of coping response will be needed to deal with a particular situation, your child might be convinced he does not have what it takes to get through it, especially when he remembers difficulties he had in the past.

Play is one of the most natural stress relievers. Taking your child outside to shoot hoops, kick a ball, or play on a swing is one of the most effective ways to teach your child how to cope and release stress.

Children can learn how to manage environmental stressors through watching parents, siblings, friends, teachers, and peers at school. If they observe people who respond to stressful situations with uncertainty, worry, nervousness, extreme caution, and overemphasis on danger, this can influence how they themselves will react, and create a pessimistic worldview.

PARENTAL INFLUENCE

First, it is important to note that most parents do not *cause* their children to be anxious; rather, they unwittingly help to perpetuate it. I say *most* parents because this statement does not hold true if there is intentional violence or abuse in the home. Sometimes in your effort to do the best you can with what you have been taught or know, you are unaware that your efforts might be hindering your children. For example, if your seven-year-old child is afraid to make new friends, you might "help" him by making the phone call to set up a playdate instead of assuring him he can get through it on his own. Parents can also affect how a child chooses to cope through his anxiety by watching the choices they make. For example, if you come home from work stressed, does your child see you reach for a glass of wine or a beer to relax? Do you yell at others and then say, "Sorry, I had a stressful day"?

Research shows that inconsistency, harsh and rigid attitudes, ambiguity, and family conflict appear to be among the primary predictors of the development of anxiety. Also identified as associated with a child's anxiety are little to no clear family rules, strong parental concern for a family's reputation, and an inability for the child to bond in infancy.

TRAUMA

Early traumatic experience can block the normal growth and development of coping skills, and affect your child's emotional and social growth.

At the time of the event, intense feelings of fear and helplessness can over-come your child, causing him to feel he cannot think clearly or function well. If your child has experienced a life event that is outside the realm of normal human experience and the associated anxiety continues over time, even with your care, concern, and discussions with him, you may want to consult with your medical provider. Please note that some symptoms of anxiety may not occur at the time of the event. In some cases, there is a delayed reaction. Also, if your child has ever experienced a panic attack and continues to avoid the place it was experienced, he is more likely to grow and learn from the experience if you seek professional help from a licensed provider. When help is delayed, it can complicate and/or prolong treatment.

Your child's reaction to trauma is affected by his age, what life has felt like so far, temperament and personality, and when the trauma happened. This can result in feelings of loss of control and stability, worry about per-sonal safety, and grief reactions. When the trauma has been long lasting or a sense of hopelessness develops, as in the case of abuse or bullying, you might see school refusal (resisting attendance) or even suicidal thinking. Trauma comes in many forms, and even if the bullying occurred one time you should notify the child's teacher, principal, and school nurse.

FOOD

If your child is malnourished or regularly eats foods containing excess sugar, additives, or caffeine, he may experience anxiety, feelings of panic, an inability to sleep, night frights, and/or depression. Improper nutrition can influence your child's thought processes by altering his ability to con-centrate or learn new material; it can also lower his level of awareness, weaken the growth process of his brain, and even increase the duration and intensity of a cold.

Because anxiety affects blood sugar levels, it can cause sensitivities and stomach problems such as pain, a bloated or distended stomach, dis-comfort, indigestion, and symptoms of hyperglycemia and hypoglycemia. When your child overeats, especially sweets and desserts, it can affect his nervous system. This can trigger moodiness, anxiousness, sleepiness, or depression. Some people have released their anxiety almost completely through a reduction of sugary or caffeinated foods and drinks.

SLEEP

A good night's sleep, as you probably know, can make a world of difference in your child's ability to handle himself. It can refuel his body's energy, give his active brain the rest it needs, and all around put him mentally in a better mood. On the flip side, a lack of sleep is known to disrupt the body's ability to replenish hormones that affect both physical and mental health. For children experiencing anxiety, poor sleep is linked to learning problems, slower emotional and physical growth, bedwetting, and high blood pressure.

Important Points to Consider

Your child may have many questions about her anxiety, one of which may be, "Why do I have anxiety problems when other people don't?" There are many different causes of anxiety and factors that contribute to it. Perhaps you and your child can easily pinpoint the source of her anxiety, or it may take some digging. As you help your child understand her anxiety, here are some thoughts to remember:

- Be aware of how you and others in your household handle your own anxiety or worry. Growing up in environments where fear, worry, and anxiety are consistently modeled by parents or family members may teach a child to be anxious.

- Life events or changes (new school, moving, loss of a loved one) can be a big cause of anxiety for your child. If possible, keep your child informed of what will take place. The more information your child has, the more prepared she will feel and this will lessen her anxiety.

- Teach your child how to restructure her thoughts from negative to positive. Positive thoughts yield positive feelings, which in turn can help your child cope with anxiety.

- A poor diet and lack of sleep can add to your child's anxiety. Encourage your child to have healthy habits to benefit her body and mind.

 **CHAPTER 4**

Signs and Symptoms of Anxiety

Children experiencing anxiety show telltale signs of the turmoil hidden below the surface. These indicators fall into several categories, but the underlying theme is that your child feels that he simply cannot meet the demands of life because they are too difficult or frightening. As a parent, you are uniquely qualified to observe your child and recognize the signs that your child is overwhelmed. Pay attention to the frequency, intensity, and duration of the behaviors in your child. In addition, the more signs your child displays, the more likely the underlying cause is anxiety. It is also helpful to keep in mind the ways that your child may seem different from his peers.

Behavioral Expressions

Because children are less likely to be able to identify and verbalize feelings of worry and anxiety, they are more likely to show anxiety through their behaviors. Keep in mind that the older your child, the more likely he will be able to talk about his internal states. Children act out feelings as a normal expression of their development, which can sometimes be frustrating. As a result, parents often mistake a child's behavioral challenges for stubbornness, laziness, or willfulness. In fact, the overall message a child experiencing anxiety communicates through behavior is a state of hopelessness.

MELTDOWNS

A meltdown can be best described as a total emotional breakdown. Your child may sob, wail, refuse to move or respond, or talk nonstop about an event he found upsetting. He may seem inconsolable, or unable to rally for the next demand, like homework, an outing, or dinnertime. Adolescents may "freak out," lamenting about issues that may seem trivial or even insensible from the adult point of view.

TEARFULNESS

Tears in response to disappointments, loss, or injury to the physical or emotional self are normal and expected in children (and adults, too!). Tears are one of the ways the body releases stress hormones, which is why many people feel better after a good cry. However, if your child is tearful for no apparent reason, cannot seem to stop crying in response to an upset, or seems to "cry at the drop of a hat," anxiety could be the underlying cause.

MINDFUL TRANSITIONS

Many children feeling anxious have difficulty switching gears between activities. This may occur at school between subjects, at particular times during the day, such as between playtime and dinner, or when a new set of skills or attention is required. A child may dawdle or show one of the behaviors discussed earlier. Many people regard transitions as the time in between or preparation for the next task. This may be true, but to ease pressure, consider your transition to *be* the experience. You might say to your child, "I notice that when I slow down and feel the weight of the book in my hands, the texture of my bag, or the texture and smell of my clothes as I put them on, it has a way of calming my mind and body." This is an aspect of mindfulness, focusing on physical details of the present moment rather than worrying about what might come next. Redirecting your child to the present moment (e.g., feeling his feet connected to the floor) with his senses is a way of providing him with tools to manage anxiety.

REQUESTS

Your child may refuse to meet requests, obligations, or deadlines. Requests such as doing his chores, getting ready for bed, or participating in family activities may be pushed away. Children who are afraid they cannot do something well, or if they feel unsure that they can meet your standards, may instead avoid the request altogether. See this as a signal that they may need some encouragement or recognition for the things they have done.

Avoidance

Avoidance is one of the hallmarks of anxiety in both adults and children. Because your child wants to shy away from what is uncomfortable, she may resist doing things that take her out of her comfort zone. Children feeling nervous or uncomfortable may avoid social situations or occasions in which they fear they will be called upon to use skills they are certain they do not possess, such as a class presentation. To avoid feeling inadequate, your child may procrastinate or even shut down entirely. Parents may respond by either pushing or coddling, or by avoiding the issue themselves. Research shows that parents of children with anxiety tend to do tasks for children or respond in a way that does not increase and encourage autonomy in the child. This increases avoidance of independence in the future because the child is blocked from experiencing an internal sense of competence or mastery.

Procrastination is a specific form of avoidance. In the moment, the child experiences a temporary relief from anxiety; however, it also sets your child up for a position of frustration and failure. Children experiencing this symptom need clear timelines and check-ins for follow-through.

Feeling Isolated

One of the most debilitating aspects of anxiety is its power to cause people to feel different, isolated, and cut off from the world. This feeling of alienation can come in many forms and tends to feed on itself. Of course, some children are naturally more introverted than others, but often feelings of being different and separate from others can lead to increased symptoms of anxiety and withdrawal. Left unaddressed, these are overpowering feelings that can lead to depression in a child with anxiety.

Children who are anxious may shy away from contact with family as well. Although it is common for teens or children who are more solitary or introverted to spend time alone in their rooms, children feeling anxious may avoid family contact more often than not. Your child may try to opt out of family outings, especially when extended family is included. He may appear to be indifferent, hang back, or be slow to warm when extended family or company is present. He may opt for solitary activity, even when the opportunity for more interesting group interaction is available.

Check in with your own motives periodically. Without realizing it, you might be pressuring your child to please you. For example, you might indirectly or directly compare the child to a sibling. Setting your child free from needing to please you or from attempting to keep up with a sibling is truly a gift to you and your child.

ALONE AT SCHOOL

Children faced with anxiety may be highly sensitive, and at times overreact to challenges, disappointments, or feel isolated in their school environment. Making and keeping friends can be challenging. This is very difficult for parents to witness. Some children may come home from school teary and overwhelmed by social demands they feel they cannot meet. Your child may make statements such as "no one likes me" or "everybody's mean to me." He may be afraid to try new things, like join a club or activity.

THEY CAN DO IT, WHY CAN'T I?

Anxiety has a way of exaggerating what children don't like about themselves. When this occurs, achievements of others may be viewed as more important than is due, and the child may downplay his own accomplishments. Fear of failure may cause anxious children to give up before they have mastered a new skill. In their mind they think, "why bother?" believing that they are unable to measure up to the expectations of their peer group. They may give up entirely on learning a new skill, like the child who becomes afraid of trying to ride a bike or apply for a part-time job because his friends have already mastered the skill. A child experiencing anxiety may believe that others accomplish things effortlessly and give up on his task, believing he is a failure because the task isn't easy. If you believe this is true for your child, try modeling persistence and/or share a story of your own frustration with mastering a skill.

Skipping School

One of the most troubling patterns that can develop in children feeling anxious is refusing to attend or stay at school. Separation anxiety, generalized anxiety, social fears, and peer issues all contribute to school avoidance. A pattern of school refusal, once established, can be extremely difficult to break and requires a team approach. Most often the team would need to include the child's teacher, parents, school nurse, and mental health professional such as a school counselor or school psychologist.

WHAT ARE THE SIGNS?

Most children who attempt to avoid school will do so by complaining of physical symptoms. Headaches, stomachaches, and vague complaints of not feeling well are common in children with anxiety. Complaining, pleading, dawdling, "disappearing," and repeated attempts to avoid or be absent from school (for example, by regularly missing the bus) are common. In these cases, gather as much information as possible. Notice any patterns, such as the child not wanting to attend school on specific days or possibly to avoid certain situations. For example, make note if any tests, projects, public speaking, or competitive activities are occurring.

WHAT ARE THE CONSEQUENCES?

The most obvious consequence of missing school is that your child may get behind in her schoolwork. For the child who is already anxious, missing homework can become overwhelming, spiraling into more physical complaints and additional attempts to avoid school. Another consequence, particularly for a child who is socially anxious, involves missed opportunities to build competence in peer interactions. The longer a child is away from school, the more daunting it becomes to go back into the fray of social demands. In this case, the proverbial "getting back on the horse after a fall" directly applies. Typically, the longer your child is away from school, the less confident and motivated she may be.

Meditation alters brain wave patterns, even among new practitioners. This means you can teach your child to focus on the moment and become aware of what is happening both inside and outside of her body so that she can change her brain from an alert, vigilant, stressed condition to a more relaxed, soothing state of mind.

WHAT CAN YOU DO?

If you feel your child attempts to stay home from school more than she should, you can use several approaches, depending on your child's particular pattern. Sometimes, friends or siblings attending the same school can be excellent supports for your child. You may wish to spend some extra time at your child's school (by volunteering, for example) if this encourages her to stay in school. However, be prepared to wean your involvement at some point so that your child can learn to tolerate being at school on her own. School nurses, psychologists, or social workers may also be called upon to help encourage a child experiencing anxiety to stay through the day.

You may also consider taking your child to a mental health provider trained in meditation, biofeedback, or guided visualization. A shift in perception first requires a shift in brain waves from the beta frequency, a more alert state, to the alpha frequency, where she can imagine herself going back to school in a more relaxed state.

Homework Hassles

Homework can be a trigger for children experiencing anxiety. They may already be feeling overwhelmed and pressured, and now they have to use their "free" time doing something that creates more stress and anxiety. At the same time, their fear of failure puts them on the wheel of frustration and cycle of perfectionism. Some children get emotionally overwrought trying to call up the attention and focus needed to complete the work. Supervision and reassurance is often required from a parent who is busy preparing a meal, or is tired from the day's demands.

Parents need to remember that they know their child best. Be an advocate for your child's learning and set realistic expectations and boundaries with teachers. For example, if your child is melting over homework you may request a decrease in the amount of homework. Children with anxiety are known for putting things off or worrying about what will happen if they don't get something done. Another way to set boundaries is to request that your child's teacher only speak to him in private. For example, if your child does not do well on a test or is having trouble in class it is best if the teacher addresses it one-on-one rather than in front of a group. These types of boundaries allow your child to feel safe being vulnerable which is critical to his emotional development.

Stress and anxiety without awareness can impinge learning, decreasing the ability to process and recall information. In the case of anxiety, as well as learning disabilities, it is better to give less homework. If your child has a true diagnosis of an anxiety disorder he will qualify for a 504 plan, which allows him to receive accommodations. If your child does not have a diagnosis it will be important for you to be sure he is not overscheduled in other areas of his life so he is able to receive adequate rest, nutrition, and downtime.

WHAT DOES IT LOOK LIKE?

Typical patterns of homework refusal may include procrastination or dawdling, forgetting assignments or materials needed to complete the work, defiance, excessive need for reassurance, and inability to work independently. Some children become great at the disappearing act by running off to a friend's house or holing up in their rooms. Some children may even offer to do chores or help with food preparation in an effort to avoid doing their homework.

WHAT CAN YOU DO TO HELP?

First, be aware of your child's assignments and obligations for school. Make checking your child's backpack or folder a daily part of your routine, such as when he first comes home from school or when you come home from work. Communicate your belief that your child can do the work on his own, but that you will be happy to assist him if he gets stuck. Become a partner with your child. Let him know that as a team you can break his school obligations into manageable bits that can be tackled and accomplished with little anxiety.

Other factors that can help with homework anxiety include:

O Turn the TV or radio off. If your child feels listening to music helps, it is best if the music is low and/or does not have words.

O Give your child time to play or exercise before homework.

O Consider limiting after-school obligations, particularly if homework is forcing your child to stay up late.

- Help your child choose an area that is well lighted, the least noisy, and clear of clutter. Have your child do homework routinely in that area, at about the same time each day.

- Have an organizational calendar (that is only for your child) in the work area to assist in long-term planning. That way your child can visually see and plan out how much time she has to complete an assignment.

- Encourage your child to hydrate and eat a healthy snack while tackling homework. Put out carrot sticks or hummus, crackers, strawberries, or other fruits for your child to graze on.

- Consider reading a book or magazine nearby so that you are available for support. You are also modeling good study habits.

- Encourage younger siblings to draw or do projects in the same area, but only if they do not overly distract your child.

- Be positive and reinforce your child's efforts.

- If homework is taking too long—meaning it is interfering with sleep, eating, and exercise—make an appointment to speak with your child's teachers.

- Encourage your child to get up, stretch, and move around in between tasks. If he experiences tension while sitting, suggest a seated spinal twist (putting hand on back of chair and gently twisting the spine in both directions). Also, neck and shoulder rolls and stretching arms overhead can renew attention.

WHEN AND HOW TO TALK TO THE TEACHER

If your child is experiencing anxiety-related concerns at school, be prepared to increase your level of contact with his teacher. Keep in mind that some teachers are more receptive than others are to emotional concerns, and it may be necessary to enlist the school social worker or other helpers to advocate for your child. When you do speak with teachers and support staff, rather than tell stories, consider describing the symptoms. For example, "Danny is showing signs of stress, nervousness, and worry about getting his math done. This has been going on for several weeks a few times a week. It appears to be impacting his ability to concentrate, sleep, and focus. I would like to speak to you about some ways we can support Danny." Generally, it is a good idea to let your child know that you plan to talk with his teacher. Some children will be embarrassed by this, as it can increase their anxiety if they feel the teacher is watching them closely. Typically with younger children, the adults (teachers and parents) speak first before including the child in on a meeting, if at all. With teens it is best to include them in a school meeting right away.

Friendship Challenges

Social difficulties can be a source of stress and trigger symptoms of anxiety in your child. Children may experience an inward conflict of wanting to fit in, yet the amount of stress it takes to fit in is overwhelming. This may in turn introduce or exacerbate a fear of failure. Feelings of alienation may or may not be an accurate assessment of the reality of the situation. Your empathy and understanding of your child's frustrations, along with your persistent and gentle encouragement, can go a long way to improving your child's social experiences. Try not to minimize the enormous power social frustration and discomfort play in a child's developing sense of independence and self-esteem.

Late elementary and early middle school (grades six through eight) years can be particularly difficult as it is normal for social cliques to develop. Cliques serve a purpose of helping children to experiment with social power and a sense of belonging; however, for those outside of the circle it can be hurtful. Consider encouraging your child to participate in activities that are less competitive. Also, both boys and girls benefit greatly from role models who illustrate how to feel and talk about their feelings comfortably, meaning without fear of being ridiculed. Children flourish in environments where their feelings are honored and accepted for what they are.

NO ONE WANTS TO PLAY WITH ME

Shyness and being quiet are common traits in children sensitive to anxiety. Initiating social interaction or including themselves in a situation where other children are already involved in an activity may at times be challenging. Your child may end up feeling that she is unwanted. Conversely, as you have already learned, peers can reject children with anxiety when their behavior is seen as immature, disruptive, or odd. Consider role-playing with your child to explore ways to handle herself in social situations (parent, role-play as your child and have your child pretend to be the other kids). Model rather than tell your child what to do and say.

Notice if your child repeats statements such as *they won't play with me* or *they hang out without me.* Encourage your child to close her eyes and visualize those thoughts being washed away in the water. Perhaps she can do this in the shower or bathtub. It can help if she gives her thoughts a color. Often these are hidden belief systems that can be cleared away through using her imagination. Without realizing it when your child worries she creates pictures in her mind. These images whether conscious or not contribute to fearful thoughts. Through creative images your child can begin to reprogram fearful thinking into a more positive outlook.

Older children may compare themselves negatively to others, and may feel they have little or nothing of value to offer as a friend. Younger children may simply feel restless or uneasy around peers for reasons they are not yet able to identify. Your child may fear doing things other more gregarious children do, such as sports, video games, or sleepovers. To help your child overcome this roadblock, encourage and reward baby steps. You can also play a game or sport with your child to help increase confidence and ability and lessen fears.

Body Talk

Homeostasis is the body's way of putting itself back into balance. For example, if your body is low on iron you may experience symptoms such as weakness and fatigue. Once you take iron supplements or eat more iron-rich foods you may feel more alert, strong, and happy. Anxiety works in the same way. It is your body's way of communicating how your child may require more play, outdoor time, sleep, healthy foods, vitamin D, and habits that allow her to receive the moment (e.g., breathing, stretching, etc.).

It is not uncommon for children sensitive to anxiety to experience and complain of physical pain and discomfort. Following are some of the symptoms most commonly experienced. Keep in mind that for stress and anxiety to be the culprit of these symptoms, they must be unrelated to sports or other injuries.

ACHES AND PAINS

Aches and pains cover a relatively diffuse variety of physical sensations. They most typically include:

O Muscle aches

O Joint pain

O Tightness or tingling, most commonly in chest or extremities

O Back and/or neck pain

If your child experiences more than one or two of the pains on this list more than once or twice a week, start with your family physician to rule out any underlying physical conditions that could be causing the discomfort. If a trusted physician rules out physical causes, it may be time to seek psychological help.

FAT TALK

Fat talk is negative statements or put-downs your child may say directly or indirectly about her body. According to Common Sense Media, "the pursuit of a perfect body is no longer a 'girl' thing. . . . Girls want to get skinny and boys want to bulk up and lose body fat." Parents can reduce body anxiety by avoiding diet language, limiting exposure to media, and avoiding purchasing magazines that emphasize outside appearance. Pay attention to what your child watches on TV or on the Internet. Try to steer your children toward activities and websites that are developmentally appropriate, value kids for who they are, and are community driven. Equally important is to know that fat talk may be code language for "I feel unworthy" or "I am under a lot of pressure." If your child talks about how fat he is, rather than say "no, you are not," ask him about what he was just doing or thinking about. Fat talk doesn't usually just appear out of nowhere; often there is something behind it. Most of all, watch how you refer to your own body. For example, notice what you say when you are looking in the mirror or trying on new clothing. Avoid habits such as weighing yourself, calling yourself fat, or reporting how much you weigh. Focus on how amazing the human body is and the importance of living a balanced lifestyle. Comments such as, "I felt so strong on my walk today," or "When I drink water I feel a difference in my energy levels" are far more effective.

Nervous Habits

Have you ever watched someone chew her fingernails, bounce her leg incessantly, twirl her hair, or snap chewing gum? These are all examples of nervous habits. Other nervous habits include knuckle-cracking, tapping fingers or objects, biting the lips, picking at the skin, or straightening clothing or other objects. Although most people have one or two nervous habits, in children these habits can go from distracting to debilitating if they are incessant. Interestingly, nervous habits develop unconsciously as a way to tame tension. If you see your child engaging in nervous habits like these, this may be a sign that she needs some exercise, fresh air, support, or a break from her present task. Refrain from judging or assuming all habits are bad. Instead, see it as feedback for you and your child about her bodily needs. If you have a nervous habit, observe yourself next time you in engage in it and see how it may interfere with your ability to breathe deeply and calm your body.

Important Points to Consider

As many children don't have the verbal dialogue to communicate their anxiety being present, noticing your child's behaviors is key to helping her deal with her anxiety.

O Your child may avoid tasks or gatherings due to her anxiety. Help your child break down tasks into small manageable steps to ease the level of anxiety they create.

O Feeling isolated or complaining that no one likes her are common signs of anxiety. Communicate with your child and try and find out why she feels this way.

O If your child is anxious about homework, make sure you help her set herself up for success by assisting in the choice of a quiet workspace, making sure she takes frequent breaks, and being there by her side in case she encounters trouble.

O Anxiety often interferes with your child making friends. If she talks to you about how she can't make friends, model how to handle the situation through role-play or by giving your child tips and talking points to start conversations.

 **CHAPTER 5**

School Days

School is one of the biggest triggers for anxiety in children. Children who may not have been sensitive to anxiety before may illustrate signs of it once they experience the social, emotional, and academic pressures of the school environment. Children may find it stressful as they attempt to conform to the academic standards and expectations. School experiences require many adjustments, some of which are expected and others which are not. Some of these include adjusting to teachers, schedules, academic expectations, friendships, homework, transitions, developmental shifts, and more. However, along the way, parents will have to listen and pay attention in order to guide their child, and in some cases advocate for situations that position the child for optimal growth.

Anxiety about School

A certain amount of anxiety about school is normal and expected. Making new friends, completing homework, taking tests, completing projects, athletic or performance schedules, and the demands of "fitting it all in" can tax even the most confident child. If your support and encouragement do not seem to help your child gain a sense of mastery, and if he loses sleep, avoids school, or worries more than you think he should, you will want to pay special attention to this chapter.

VALUES REDUCE ANXIETY

According to author Mark Waldman, "reflecting on personal values can keep neuroendocrine and psychological responses to stress at low levels." By clearly communicating your values (e.g., respect) as opposed to repeating your rules and expectations, you can encourage your child without stressing him out. Most children truly want to do the right thing and please their parents. However, when parents constantly restate the rules this can send a message that you don't trust or believe in the abilities of your child. Consider having a brief yet meaningful conversation about your values rather than quick, impulsive reminders about your rules. This can be done at a family meeting time (not dinner) when you and your family can briefly sit together without distractions.

HOME STUDY

The word "homework" may itself be an anxiety trigger for your child, as it implies more work. Parents may want to adopt their own language when asking about homework, instead referring to it as home study or studies. Also be mindful of your own statements and attitude toward homework. If you speak of the "dreaded homework," your child will pick up on this and begin to sing the same tune. Often these statements are a sign that a parent needs to communicate to the teacher about the amount or intensity of the workload. Speaking to teachers does not mean you are attempting to change them or get them to agree with your viewpoint. It is an opportunity to provide constructive feedback about your child, and in many cases parents walk away with a renewed perspective or reassurance from the teacher.

Expecting Anxiety

There are times when your child may be expecting anxiety. When he assumes he is outside his safe zone, and fears he will not be able to handle the situation without panic, this can also create anxiety. Sometimes referred to as the "fear of fear," the overall goal is really to avoid distressing feelings. The anxiety your child feels when thinking about the feared event increases his tendency to avoid it, and magnifies feelings of distress if the situation actually does occur. You can help your child by encouraging him to become an advocate for himself, to ask questions about what is happening, offer viewpoints, and inquire about his choices. For example, if your child is nervous about taking a certain class, ask him about what he expects, what he is dreading, and the choices he believes he has before brainstorming solutions.

Test Anxiety

Almost all children will experience test anxiety at some time in their school careers. Small to moderate levels of anxiety actually increase performance, while more severe amounts cause performance to drop off. Test anxiety occurs when strong or unpleasant emotions interfere with your child's ability to absorb, retain, and recall information. Anxiety creates a kind of "mental static" in the brain, which interferes with learning, memory, and the ability to reason and think clearly. Feelings such as worry, fear, and frustration actually derail the central nervous system, causing it to get out of rhythm, thereby disrupting mental processes. Conversely, positive feelings like hope and appreciation lead to increased balance and harmony in the nervous system. This enhances performance and creates positive emotional pathways, building on success.

Many children with anxiety believe they don't have a voice. Encourage your child to use his voice in a more mature way. Allow your child to have opinions, challenge ideas, and negotiate solutions in a calm way. Of course, you still have the final say in what is negotiable and what is non-negotiable.

BE PREPARED

One of the most basic approaches to managing test anxiety is to help your child maximize his sense of competence by ensuring preparation for an exam. You may wish to help by using practice questions or by encouraging him to review with friends. The younger your child is, the easier it may be to make a game out of this.

According to Kelly McGonigal in *The Upside of Stress*, "Recent research suggests stress doesn't hurt performance on tests and can even help. People who feel anxious during a test may actually do better." If your child is anxious about taking a test, embrace it. Encourage him to see the stress as motivation for a higher performance.

How your child prepares for the review is also important. Productive study skill habits such as effective note taking, organization, and time management set your child up for success. You and your child may ask the teacher for a study guide. Encourage your child to talk out loud when he studies, similar to how an actor remembers his lines (using flexion in his voice). Some children do better when they are permitted to move their bodies or listen to background music. Be sure your child gets enough sleep and nutrition during exam time.

Counter Negative Rehearsal

Negative rehearsal or mental repetition of negative thoughts and fears is actually what drives anticipatory anxiety. The repeated negative thoughts about the feared event engrave anxiety responses, creating an endless loop and making the situation seem unbearable. As a parent it will be important to watch for counterproductive language. For example, if your child says, "I hate tests," help him to see tests are an opportunity to review, strengthen, and show what you know about a subject. If your child is not agreeable to seeing tests as opportunities, ask him to imagine the word "hate" drifting down a river and away from him. What your child does not realize is that these types of words and statements actually prevent him from showing his knowledge. You can also encourage your child to imagine himself getting up, going to school, entering the classroom where the test will occur, taking, and finishing the test with ease. Through relaxation and visualization your child can begin to view himself successfully moving through, rather than being paralyzed by, difficult situations.

Older children may purchase an app for relaxation where they visualize to soothing sounds. Your child can also state a mantra for himself. For example, he can repeat out loud to himself, "Taking tests comes naturally and easy for me" ten consecutive times per day. For teens who may feel this is silly, you can let them know techniques such as these are used in sports psychology by professional athletes to prepare them for their mental game. Like children, even the best athletes get performance anxiety.

Stories and encouragement about your own experiences with nervousness (taking a driving test, for example) can be helpful. Be sure to include what you have learned from the process (perhaps the way you thought about yourself and others) and try not to overstate your teaching points. Stories are best when delivered with lightness, and maybe even laughter.

TAPPING

Tapping is a technique based on the principles of acupressure. Certain points on the body are tapped lightly over and over using the tips of the finger while making statements such as, "Even though I feel anxious about my test I completely and totally accept myself." This technique moves emotional charges—strong reactions your child feels when he keeps revisiting the same thoughts over and over again. Tapping helps break up the density of emotion, allowing the energy to move freely rather than becoming static in the body. When tapping is done for several minutes, your child will eventually receive relief from the tension brought upon by the emotional charge. One of the points is called the karate chop and is located on the outside of the hand halfway between the bottom of the pinky and the bottom of the hand. Before teaching tapping to children, try tapping on yourself first. The next time you feel an emotional charge, close your eyes and tap that point while repeating aloud, "Even though I feel _____, I completely and totally accept myself." The tapping session can take anywhere from three to five minutes.

TOUCHSTONES

Have you ever found yourself toying with change or keys in your pocket, or twisting a ring on your finger? If so, you are using a touchstone to calm yourself. A touchstone is an object that your child carries with her that she can touch or hold, which becomes grounding and comforting for her. It should be small enough to be worn or carried, and be an object that has a symbolic or emotional meaning for your child. Examples include smooth stones, coins, crystals, small amulets or figurines, jewelry, or key rings. Help your child to find an object she can carry with her to use like this when anxious or upset. Often items children find in nature, such as a smooth rock, will work well. Encourage your child to use her touchstone while she practices other skills such as breathing or imagery to reduce both testing and general anxiety.

Crystals give off an electromagnetic frequency. Many children experiencing anxiety feel weak in their ability to cope with stress and negativity. By carrying a rock, mineral, or crystal in their pocket, they can add to and increase their own personal vibration. When vibration is low, you may feel drained. However, when vibration is high, resiliency increases. Teach your child to go for natural resources rather than synthetic stimulants such as soda to rebalance her body.

Handling Anxiety at School

Many children choose to push through their day at school, collapsing or melting at the end of the day, never really knowing they are experiencing symptoms of anxiety. Transitions are a great time for your child to utilize techniques such as deep breathing, stretching, yawning (a built-in stress reliever), drinking water, playing, reading, drawing, and reconnecting mind and body by engaging her larger muscles (legs and thighs). Children can try tapping or they can even do energy techniques such as rubbing their hands together vigorously and then hovering the palm of one hand (with their fingers closed) over their heart center (2 inches above) for three breaths (inhale and exhale equals one breath), and then over their midsection (navel area) for three breaths, in front of their throat for three breaths, and finally over their forehead for three breaths.

Techniques such as these don't magically make the symptoms disappear. However, they can tone down the intensity of anxiety symptoms enough so that your child can recognize and observe her thoughts without feeling overwhelmed or threatened by them. The calmer your child feels (which is the purpose of breathing techniques, for example), the more likely she is able to observe her thoughts without following them, meaning she is able to think a fearful thought without personalizing or making it her current reality. She can see that she has a choice to keep thinking the same thoughts or to interrupt the cycle by yawning or laughing. Even a fake sneeze can redirect her attention to more uplifting or kind ways of thinking. After all thoughts are just thoughts, and most of the time they stem from the past or future. When your child chooses to focus on the ones that give her information about the here and now, she is learning and growing from her experiences with anxiety.

Parents can help their children by discussing how they might de-stress during the day. Talk about how you had a stressful moment at work or the grocery store, and what you did to restore calm and balance in your body. Open the dialogue between you and your child by asking, "How do you help yourself through the stress in your day?" Parents and children can learn a lot from each other.

LUNCHTIME MOANS

The social melting pot of your child's lunchroom can be overwhelming if she is especially sensitive, introverted, or self-conscious. If your child is unable to eat around others, you will want to address this early. Enlist school personnel and a therapist who can help with a plan of gradual exposure so that your child can learn how to thrive from managing fears rather than be overcome by them. This requires building confidence bit by bit. For example, the school can help your child by finding familiar lunch partners or a regular table. It is helpful when adults and teachers take a moment to check in with students. Schools may even prepare a list of conversation topics, and alternative lunch space may be an option where some children meet in a smaller group setting to practice basic conversational skills. Your child may prefer a lunch brought from home as opposed to waiting in line to purchase a prepared meal, which can be anxiety-provoking as children may worry there will be no place for them to sit.

Family meals are a great opportunity to foster consciousness and awareness. Gathering as a family unit promotes a sense of connection and unity, two key factors in strengthening self-awareness. Be sure to stay true to these family traditions by instilling rules such as no cell phones at the table or television in the background.

STAYING IN CLASS

If your child has trouble staying in class and has frequent urges to leave, this may be a sign that she is choosing to run from her symptoms of anxiety. This is a temporary fix and will only increase her feelings of panic and hopelessness. Teach your child not to be afraid of her tension. The impulse to leave is often a response to bodily tension, which in some cases is simply memory of irritation or fear that may be stored in the body. The body is highly intelligent and holds memory just like your brain does. Explain tension to your child as an intersection. Imagine seeing someone wanting to cross the street. Imagine waving to the person to go ahead and cross before you drive through the intersection. It is the same thing with tension. When your child feels it in her body she can simply say to the tension in her mind, "Okay, you go first, then me." This teaches children to pause and allow tension to move through and past them, rather than react to it. It will also be important to look at your child's diet to evaluate the amount of sweets and stimulants she may be consuming, and to cut down on them if necessary. Nutritional supplements that promote calm and relaxation may also be beneficial.

TRANSITIONS

Some transitions are anticipated, while others are not. Your child will benefit from you giving her a heads-up for transitions that are expected, as well as creating coping strategies for the unexpected. For example, your child might experience a pop quiz, fire drill, or substitute teacher, or something that she thought was going to happen may be canceled. Once your child is equipped with strategies like tapping, touchstones, and mindfulness, she can then apply them to these unexpected moments.

Peers and Peer Pressure

The demands of social interaction can be especially traumatic for children who are experiencing high anxiety, who worry more, and are exceedingly shy or self-conscious. In fact, it is not uncommon for children with anxiety to have difficulty making, keeping, and interacting with friends.

A child experiencing anxiety (even if it is situational, such as during a parents' divorce) may display anxiety socially rather than at home with you. The child may have previously appeared to be socially comfortable but is now experiencing some fear of rejection. Regardless of where and when the anxiety shows up, the tools, strategies, and resources remain the same. Keep in mind that one of the greatest ways to support children is through active listening. Listen with full attention, without the distractions of phones, household tasks, and computers.

PEER PRESSURE

You have no doubt had firsthand experience with peer pressure, especially during your adolescent years. Peer pressure can add to insecurity and undermine self-confidence. As your child grows older, family influences take a back seat to those of his peer group. His circle of friends influences what he wears, watches, listens to, eats, believes in, and aspires to. Because children are trying to fit in at the same time that they are learning to express themselves, the pressure to conform can become an easy solution to identity confusion. For socially anxious children, peer pressure may be especially powerful, with its promise of "safety in numbers." You can support your child by helping him talk about peer pressure, especially about any influences he finds confusing or distasteful. It may help to ask, "How would you feel about a person who does/thinks _____? Would you want that person as a friend?"

THE IMPORTANCE OF ANCHORING

Your child's symptoms are a reminder of how important it is that he be connected and supported. Activities such as sports, dance, Scouts, martial arts, drama, choir or band, and church youth groups can all provide your child with a basic sense of security in the social world. They are ready-made opportunities for finding friends who share similar interests and schedules. Hopefully, other children in these specialized peer groups will be a positive influence on his attitudes and behavior, encouraging him to stretch socially. You might try carpooling or hosting a small gathering for his group to encourage your child to use new skills. Take pride and show interest in his choices by attending events or performances, or by volunteering to help if you can.

Bullies and Gossip

It's estimated that as many as 20 to 30 percent of children have been bullied at some time, and that bullying is most common in the middle-school years. The effects of bullying and gossip can even be harmful to those merely observing it. It was previously believed that bullies lacked self-esteem and put others down to gain self-confidence. However, recent findings show that bullies are more confident than previously thought, but that they tend to lack empathy, are poor communicators, and may be raised in homes where aggression is an acceptable response to conflict.

Gossip is verbal bullying, to which girls often resort. It can include name-calling, rumors, and lies, and can have devastating effects, particularly for a child who is already anxious socially. A child who struggles with anxiety may feel she has no recourse, and the powerlessness may lead to avoidance, isolation, and depression. If you suspect your child is the victim of bullying or gossip, listen supportively and try the following:

- Encourage your child to practice "safety in numbers."
- Help your child to widen her social circle.
- Role-play ways to ignore and walk away from teasing or pestering.
- Role-play saying no and being assertive.
- Involve the school if violence, racial slurs, or serious threats of harm occur.

Middle-School Meltdowns

Middle school can be one of the most socially tumultuous times for children. Brains are rewiring and hormones are surging, and children at this age compete for social status, which can sometimes change rapidly. If your child is already having difficulty with worry and panic, this developmental transition can be extremely painful, and making sure therapy is available is important.

A hallmark of this age is the clique, a social group that is highly exclusive and demands strict conformity. The clique usually has a "ringleader" or "queen bee," and members see themselves as superior to others outside the group. Those who do not belong can feel inferior, and even threatened, as the clique can have great social power.

SOCIAL SUPPORT

Many elementary and middle schools offer "friendship groups" for children who are awkward or have social anxiety, or who are new to the school. Usually, a school social worker leads the groups, in addition to providing individual support to children in the school district. Groups usually meet weekly or bimonthly, and most children look forward to breaks from class and an opportunity to build friendship skills. Other social connections at school may be available through mentoring, student government, peer support, or tutoring. Check with your child's school if you think he might benefit from some of these opportunities.

Staying Connected and Getting Involved

Throughout the book, you are encouraged to form a support team to help you become strong and confident in your own parenting abilities. If your child has school-based anxiety, it will be especially important to make and keep regular contact with various professionals at his school, and to support him by becoming more active in his educational experience.

If you feel that your child's teacher is not receptive to your child's needs or your requests, respectfully involve other support people, such as the nurse, social worker, psychologist, or principal. You know your child best; trust what you feel and advocate when needed. Being a conscious parent doesn't always mean you will be popular. Handle it with respect and you are more likely to feel confident in your decisions.

WHERE DO YOU START?

If your child is experiencing anxiety-related concerns at school, the once- or twice-yearly conference will likely be inadequate to address his emotional needs. Your concerns for your child are important, and no doubt feel urgent. However, remember that the teacher has many students to attend to, and to respect the teacher's needs with regard to communication. Some teachers prefer to use e-mail; others may have reserved times to speak with parents about concerns over the phone. Many are happy to schedule meetings before or after school.

CLASSROOM VOLUNTEERING

Many schools depend on volunteers to increase cooperation between families and schools, and to help things run smoothly. Volunteer opportunities vary from heading the Parent Teacher Organization to coordinating fund drives or correcting weekly spelling tests. If you become involved and interested in your child's school experience, his investment and motivation in school may improve as well. However, if you are concerned that your child might be clingy or tearful if you are there, or if your own anxiety causes you to hover or be overprotective, your child might do better without your presence. If you are unsure, talk over the options with your child's teacher or therapist to see what they might recommend.

SCHOOL EVENTS

Chaperoning one of your child's field trips or volunteering at school events can be a great way to learn more about your child's social world and about his daily struggles with anxiety. You may want to volunteer for field trips if your child has trouble managing them without you. However, you will also need to have a plan to decrease your participation so that your child can eventually experience independence. If volunteerism is especially popular in your child's school, you may have to speak up early. If joining a field trip is important for your child, you may have to travel separately, or arrange to share parts of the field trip with other parents.

Important Points to Consider

While many children are anxious about school, some children experience overwhelming symptoms of anxiety. You know your child best—keep an eye out for symptoms that indicate some aspect of school is influencing your child's emotional well-being. Keep in mind:

O Be aware that the way you talk about homework or tests influences your child's perception. Try to model positive behaviors.

O You can give your child techniques to calm himself during the school day, such as tapping, deep breathing, or carrying a touchstone.

O Talk to your child's teacher if the social scene at school is a cause for anxiety. He may have ideas for helping your child feel more comfortable.

O Though your child is away at school, there are still ways for you to stay connected to him and help ease his anxiety. Try volunteering in his class or chaperoning field trips. Talk to your child's teacher about what he thinks may be appropriate.

 **CHAPTER 6**

Outside Pressures and Influences

Outside pressures are influences that may intensify symptoms of anxiety in your child. Some of these include: cyberbullying, media, technology, fearful messaging and marketing, security warnings, and exposure to violence. The more you are aware of these outside pressures, the more you can help your child learn to put them in perspective.

Coping with Outside Pressures

Outside pressures are anything that influences your child outside of what she is exposed to within the family. Media, technology, and peer pressure are a few examples. About 50 percent of the behavior you see particularly in early childhood is developmental in nature, meaning it is normal and will pass. The remaining 50 percent is due to outside influences.

Most children will experience some levels of anxiety during certain developmental periods of their life. For example, anything that is referred to as a "first"—first dance, first game, or first time being left alone—all evoke some level of stress necessary for motivation and growth. Outside pressures have a different feel. There is no "first" and then you grow and move on. Often these pressures are ingrained into the culture, and therefore it is critical that children and families instill mindsets, boundaries, and tools that can support them through a lifetime.

According to psychiatrist Gary Small and Gigi Vorgan in their book *iBrain*, "today's obsession with computer technology and video gaming appears to be stunting frontal lobe development in many teenagers, impairing their social and reasoning abilities." Part of consciously attending to anxiety involves setting boundaries surrounding screen time and outlining consequences for overusing technology. Read *iRules*, by Janelle Burley Hoffman for ideas on setting technology limits.

BENEFITS AND RISKS OF TECHNOLOGY

When used correctly, technology can have many benefits, including quick and easy access to learning tools, research, equal opportunity for individuals with special needs, quick and easy communication, facts, ease of access to information, supportive causes, and connection to individuals/organizations that promote tolerance, empathy, and cross-culture involvement.

However, when overused, or used as a pastime or habit, technology and media can increase aggression, decrease empathy and social skill development, weaken face-to-face communication (an essential skill for healthy relationships), decrease physical activity, increase obesity, discourage personal development, instill fears, disrupt sleep, promote isolation, increase at-risk behavior such as violence, addictive behavior, and most of all increase anxiety.

Media

The term *media* refers to communication through television, radio, news, movies, newspapers, Internet (includes blogs, videos, audio files), photos (images), and commercials. Often messages of values are embedded into the stories, advertisements, and entertainment. Before the Internet, stories were targeted specifically to individuals in a certain area, meaning a newspaper and radio program could only reach so far. Now the power of the Internet has the capacity to reach billions of people with stories and content that may or may not pertain to the person who receives it.

Research shows television and computer viewing before bedtime can hinder sleep. Bedtime routines that include wind-down activities, such as a shower, bath, drawing, and reading are encouraged. Quieting (or shutting down) household noises like music and television at least an hour before bed fosters conscious living as well as a good night's sleep.

COMMERCIALS

Marketers are masterminds at subliminally influencing the likes, dislikes, values, opinions, tastes, and preferences of the consumer. Many times the commercials are more captivating than the show itself. Even the well-intentioned parent who carefully chooses the current program being viewed needs to stay alert to messages and violent images that occur before, during, and after the program. If your child is watching a DVD, it is best to fast-forward through advertisements and commercials. Otherwise, turn the volume down or switch the channel, and let your child know why you are taking action. This is an opportunity to restate your values. For example, "That commercial portrays women as objects, making it seem that being sexy is more important than intelligence, values, and self-worth, so I am going to change the channel for a moment." You might also say, "That word he used and his tone of voice were not okay." On the other hand, when you view a commercial that is appropriate and supports what you believe, make a positive comment. The rule of thumb is that what you pay attention to grows and is reinforced. In other words, give the positive more verbal attention than the negative.

BLOGS

A blog is a journal or diary that is on the Internet. A blogger is the person who keeps and writes the blog. This person can be a professional or a nonprofessional of any age who shares her news, passions, and information. The positive side to blogging is that it allows self-expression, can contribute to good causes, and spreads information that readers may not otherwise receive through the general media. The negative side is that the information may not always be true, is often subjective, and in some cases may have alternative agendas such as selling products or swaying people to support a viewpoint. If your child is reading blogs or blogging himself, it will be important for you to monitor his activity. In order to do this, it is essential that you develop clear, consistent rules and guidelines early on.

The American Psychological Association (APA) and the American Pediatric Association recommend no more than two hours of screen time per day. If you find this challenging, you may want to build in screen-free times during the course of the day. For example, you might have a rule that the car is a screen-free zone with the exception of long trips.

VIDEO GAMES

Children can play video games on the computer, phones, iPods, or via consoles such as the Wii, PlayStation, and Xbox. Some of the most popular video games are extremely violent and disturbing. A 2010 review by psychologist Craig A. Anderson and others concluded that "The evidence strongly suggests that exposure to violent video games is a causal risk factor for increased aggressive behavior, aggressive cognition, and aggressive affect and for decreased empathy and prosocial behavior." Parents need to view and research games themselves before allowing a child to play them, and not assume that a PG rating means there is no violent material. For advice and guidance on video games, movies, and other forms of media go to *www.commonsensemedia.org*.

Guidelines for Technology and Media

Children may revert to technology as a way to escape their feelings. This places them at a disadvantage as they learn to disregard, suppress, and in some cases shove away a part of themselves that stimulates inner growth. By doing so, they are likely to miss opportunities to acquire new skills that will ultimately deepen their sense of self. The following guidelines allow your child to safely experiment with technology and be exposed to media without sacrificing values, brain development, social and emotional skills, health, and overall growth.

- Unless your child needs a cell phone for safety or communication with parents, consider putting off the purchase until a child is more mature, or at the very least in middle school.

- Set rules and guidelines before items are purchased. Consider writing a contract with specific guidelines and consequences. Keep the contract short but to the point; this will increase the chance that you will follow through. Write the contract using positive phrasing, focusing on the behavior you would like to see rather than the one you are trying to prevent. For example, rather than stating "No phones during dinner," state "Phones off during meals."

- Create tech-free times that also cover accepting phone calls and texts. Create times that are negotiable, and ones that are non-negotiable. For example, phones and texting during meal-times would be non-negotiable. Using the phone first thing out of bed in the morning would be negotiable.

O Teach children that tech time includes all time spent in front of a screen. This includes TV, computer, movies, video games, and phone. Teach children how to monitor their own time. Often the hardest part for children is motivating themselves to turn it off. When they are young, provide a five- or ten-minute warning before you will turn it off. You can also use a kitchen timer as a way to remind younger children when to turn it off. As they get older, have them watch the clock or use the timer themselves. Thank them for the times they turn it off on their own. If they are unable to turn it off on their own, then the logical consequence will be that you get to be in charge of turning it off. (Note that children will test you on this; it will be important not to assume they have mastered the skill once they do it a few times.)

O Create tech-free zones. Establish early on in which areas of the home computers and cell phones may be used. Tech-free bedrooms are an excellent way to keep your child safe and to ensure that he is not using technology as a means for coping with stress.

O If children are not asking for it, refrain from suggesting it. Parents have habits as well. Notice if when your child starts whining or complaining your first response is to quickly soothe him by handing him a phone or video game. Model the behavior you wish your child to display.

O Teach cell phone and computer etiquette. No matter what your child chooses to do as a career, he will stand out if he can show self-restraint and etiquette when using technology. For example, teach children never to answer a phone or text at a dinner table. Keep cell phones off at the table. Excuse yourself politely to a private location if you need to make or receive a call. Avoid answering your phone when you are being waited on or served. It is just plain rude. Keep your voice down in public so other people don't have to hear your business. Teaching etiquette also reduces the likelihood your child will utilize technology as a means for coping with his symptoms of anxiety.

O Be an example. If you want your children to make safe choices, you need to model these choices. For example, pull over the car before texting something, and watch your own habits such as checking e-mails or surfing online as a pastime. Illustrate the importance of face-to-face contact by small acts such as putting away your phone when you greet your child or take him somewhere such as a playground, or on errands. Your smile has the potential to reduce anxiety in yourself and others.

O Watch television with your child so you can explain what is real and what is imagined, particularly for younger children (under age nine). Point out healthy behaviors when it comes to stress reduction, and also point out unhealthy behaviors.

O Watch your family habits. Do you or your children check your e-mails, texts, or play video games out of boredom? Some of these habits may actually be perpetuating the cycle of anxiety as they keep you from ever really experiencing the present moment. The next time you have this urge, choose to close your eyes and imagine feeling a warm breeze on your face. Practices such as these will teach you how to *be*, rather than *be busy* in the moment.

O Expose children to scams. If you receive an e-mail that looks fishy, show your child what it looks like. Teach them to never open e-mails from strangers or provide private information over the Internet.

O Value the development of your child's inner voice. The goal is to guide your child toward self-regulation, balancing time on and off technology. For example, if your child is looking out the window while playing on the computer this could be his inner voice saying, "Hey go out and play."

O Notice if your parental stress is due to technology itself, or rather a response to your own fear. Some parents avoid asking their children to stop because they fear conflict. What you avoid persists and many times escalates. Choose to respect yourself by sticking to your guidelines.

O Know your child's passwords as a safety precaution.

Social Media

Social media is a virtual community and network where individuals share and exchange information. Psychologists have growing concerns about the limited face-to-face contact involved, and how this may be impacting children and adolescents' identity and self-esteem. According to Howard Gardner, a Harvard psychologist who studied under psychologist and specialist in child development Erik Erikson, states, "Kids feel pushed into developing a public identity early, and since it has been widely posted and effectively branded, it is actually difficult to explore other forms of identity."

Researchers Mick Krasner and Ronald Epstein did a study with physicians through the University of Rochester School of Medicine and Dentistry. They looked at mindful ways professionals could process the stress of their work. Rather than shut down to the emotional suffering of others, they taught them to be more fully present and accept the sensations that showed up. They found physicians who did this technique were less emotionally drained and more ready to face another day. Rather then spend their time attempting to reduce stress they embraced it. (*The Upside of Stress*)

Help your child navigate the social media world by waiting until the child is at least thirteen years old (a Facebook requirement). Once on social media, keep your child in activities that help him engage with life, people, and the present moment. Teach your child to avoid going on social media sites when he is angry, sad, or upset about something. These emotional states increase the chance that he might say something he could regret. Since children experiencing anxiety may feel they are alone or they may have a fear of what others think of them it will be important for you to monitor your child's online behavior. Behaviors such as passing photos may temporarily make your child feel good but in the long run they may put themselves at risk as what gets sent into the virtual world never really goes away. Posting hurtful comments, gossip, and inappropriate content such as swearing and sexual behavior all contribute to the shaping of your child's identity, and could come at a cost later in life. On the other hand, when used appropriately, it can be a great way to market your ideas, strengths, connect with others, and send positive messages out into the world.

Boundaries

Media and technology enable people to be contacted and connected at any time of day (even if it is two o'clock in the morning). Establishing boundaries early on will not only keep your child safe, but also allow time for the self-care and attention required for relieving stress and anxiety. When possible, encourage your child to avoid group texts. A group text is received by everyone in the group, even if the current conversation is not actively involving your individual child. This can be distracting, and has the potential to pull your child away from other activities. Boundaries include teaching web safety. For example, if your child does go into a chat group, then he should never use his real name. Nor should he ever give personal information out such as name, address, and phone number.

Be sure you and your child carve out time each day to do something for yourselves. Exercise, rest, make a healthy meal, get outside, visit face-to-face with neighbors and friends, draw, paint, and attend community events. It is experiences such as these that teach your child how to enjoy people and help him stay in touch with what is happening in real time, this exact moment, the place where anxiety does not exist.

THE POWER OF "NO"

Initially, your child may feel compelled to answer every text or message that comes her way. Without guidance, children and adolescents can get into the habit of putting the needs of others first. Allowing your child to say "no," both in and outside the tech world, decreases the likelihood that she will serve as prey, or feed the insecurities of others. The ability to say "No thanks," "I will connect with your later," or "I am unable to do that" is a sign of strength.

ONLINE PREDATORS

Online predators are individuals with ulterior motives who prey on children and adolescents with insecurities, who are isolated, depressed, unsupervised, and/or emotionally needy. Parents of children with anxiety may hesitate to discuss the dark side of the Internet; however, children who are unaware are more likely to fall victim. Give your child the facts without going into details. Explain there are individuals who use the Internet as a way to entrap children, meaning they will pretend to be your friend, have similar likes, dislikes, and be willing to listen and be there for you when you need it. They may even offer you money or to buy you things. You may want to include a clause in your Internet contract stating that your child will never give his personal information (such as full name, address, age, passcodes, bank information, credit card, telephone number) to anyone he does not know. If someone or a website requests personal information he should check with you, but most likely will still never provide it.

Cyberbullying

No longer does bullying only happen on the playground, or during unstructured times such as commuting to and from school. Bullying can also happen right in a child's bedroom, online, with more than one bully at a time. If your child is being made fun of, harassed, tormented, teased, or gossiped about via social media, these would be examples of cyberbullying and could very well be the cause of his anxiety. All it takes is one instance to be enough to provoke a significant amount of fear and anxiety in a child. If this occurs, be sure to respond calmly, tell your child not to respond to the attack, then print and save the evidence. If you know the individual and feel safe doing so, you may address the problem face-to-face. In some cases, you may need to file a police report. If your child is a witness to cyberbullying, it can be equally disturbing and may show up in a child's behavior such as irritability, nervousness, and isolation. Trust your gut as a parent. If your child seems off, do not hesitate to check what is happening with social media.

Other Influences

Children today are growing up in a world of warnings. Media is constantly warning people about certain foods and how they may cause cancer, or how they might be bad for you. There are security warnings with images shown at airports, and constant exposure to reports of the violence happening all over the world. There are also warnings about germs, potentially contracting diseases, the dangers of bugs, mosquitoes, environmental toxins, and so forth. It is no wonder that anxiety is on the rise among both adults and children. It is important for your child to be knowledgeable about the influences of the world. However, the way your child responds will depend a great deal on how it is delivered.

Andrew K. Przybylski and Netta Weinstein of the University of Essex conducted a study that illustrated how phones can hurt our close relationships. Simply having a phone nearby, without even checking it, can be detrimental to our attempts at interpersonal connection. Being conscious about where you place your cell phone while spending time with your child or teen can make a difference.

Children often hear your tone and feel your anxiety more so than the actual words you are speaking. To pass on information in a calm way, parents will want to learn how to take information in, let it settle, and allow one inhalation and one exhalation (a full breath cycle) before repeating it verbally, if immediately sharing the information is necessary. This may take approximately twenty seconds. A visualization such as this one can also help you take a moment to compose yourself. Picture yourself throwing a stone into a pond. Watch the rings on the water appear and circle outward. As the rings get bigger know that they represent you truly experiencing your feelings rather than reacting to them. After about twenty seconds notice how your thoughts and sense of urgency may have changed. Sensitive information is best delivered in a calm, brief (factual), and clear way. If it is brought on too strong, then your child will focus on your reaction more than the actual information you are attempting to convey. The intent is to help your child feel guided and informed rather than overpowered by the knowledge.

Building Face-to-Face Social Skills

One of the best ways to build resiliency in your child is to help her develop face-to-face social skills. Communication is much more than abbreviated words or sentences. When you communicate face-to-face, you learn the skill of reading body language, tone of voice, and expression. Face-to-face communication tends to be more empathic, conscious, and heartfelt. Adolescents who predominately communicate through texting and social media never really learn vital communication skills, such as expressing feelings, eye contact, listening, taking turns, conflict resolution, problem solving, and how to be vulnerable with another human being. Instead, they may develop a false persona based on a need to fit in, be liked, accepted, and popular. Anxiety lives off false and negative perceptions. By becoming comfortable with herself and knowing what the symptoms of anxiety are attempting to communicate, your child will naturally gravitate toward relationships that strengthen rather than weaken her sense of self.

Here are some ways to build healthy social skills:

O Family meals are the best way to practice skills such as eye contact, taking turns, vulnerability (through stories of making mistakes), news, and interests.

O Be a model. When speaking with your child model eye contact, refrain from multitasking, ask questions, and most of all listen without interrupting.

- Provide opportunities for unstructured play. Have your child invite a friend over. Set the rule ahead of time that technology will not be a part of the playdate.

- Play family board games. Board games reinforce taking turns, waiting, following the rules, and problem solving. Family games encourage laughter, a sign your child is feeling comfortable being herself.

- Refrain from doing things for your child because you know she is feeling nervous or anxious. For example, avoid ordering your child's food for her at a restaurant, or calling your child's friend to cancel a playdate. Instead, be confident in your child's abilities.

- Make mistakes safe. Children who feel stressed or anxious may find themselves stating things they don't mean, being overly self-conscious, or socially awkward. Share your stories of mishaps and awkwardness. Know that social skill development is a lifelong journey.

- Role-play. Your child can ease anxiety by practicing ahead of time. Role-playing can be done with another person or alone in front of a mirror. For example, a child may role-play how she might handle situations that trigger anxiety. For example: how to say no, speak in front of others, ask someone to come over and play, or join a group. Children love to do skits. Many groups such as Scouts and church groups will make skits part of their curriculum. These are all opportunities to practice overcoming, and be empowered by experiencing, anxiety.

Important Points to Consider

Technology and media are useful and beneficial facets of modern society, but in terms of your child with anxiety they can also be riddled with potential pitfalls. As a parent the best thing you can do for your child is set boundaries in terms of use of technology, and try to give your child a sense of your values in regards to technology. In this way your child can be protected while at the same time being allowed to make her own decisions with the framework of values you have built.

- Media and technology constantly bombard your child with negative messages and warnings, which can increase anxiety. Teach your child how to tell truth from fiction in media, and how to unplug from it.

- As a family it is pivotal that you instill mindsets, boundaries, and tools in regards to technology that can support your child through a lifetime.

- Check your own technology habits. Are you able to unplug yourself to be there for your child? Do you always have your phone on your person? Model the behaviors you want to see reflected in your child.

- Teach your child about the downfalls and dangers of technology. Often parents of children with anxiety shy away from warning their children of predators or scams, but your child's anxiety will be lessened if he knows what to look out for and what to avoid.

- Build your child's resiliency through face-to-face social skills. Unlike technology, face-to-face communication allows your child to feel comfortable in who she really is, not a false front personality that people build on social media.

- When communicating with your child, keep in mind that children often hear your tone and feel your anxiety more than the actual words you are speaking. To pass on information in a calm way, take information in, let it settle, allow one inhalation and one exhalation (a full breath cycle), and then share the information.

 **CHAPTER 7**

Building a Supportive Home Environment

Your home is the foundation of your child's physical, emotional, and spiritual well-being. The attitudes and influences you provide as parents are the basis for your child's identity, self-esteem, coping, and worldview. These influences begin in your child's early years and are combined with experiences outside of your home. Together, they form the values and expectations that will guide your child throughout her lifetime. The conscious and supportive home environment you provide will help to decrease anxiety and increase inner calm for the entire family.

Open Communication

Communication is the basis of all relationships. It involves not only what you say to others but also the ability to listen to and observe yourself. As you and your child learn about anxiety you will see how thoughts impact how you feel and communicate with others. A large part of your child working through his symptoms will be for him to recognize his thoughts and identify which thoughts enhance communication and which ones disrupt it. Often symptoms of anxiety bring on defensive or reactive thoughts. For example, a child may inwardly fear failure and show this through defensive remarks. The behaviors of children and adolescents who communicate with intensity and/or fear ("Hurry up, Mom, or you'll make me late and I'll get in trouble with my teacher!") are often built on self-limiting belief systems. Belief systems such as *I have to fight for what I want* or *it is wrong to make a mistake* often support these kinds of behaviors. Parents can support their children by asking their child what they believe to be true. For example, "What do you believe will happen if you are late?" Once your child has identified what he thinks will happen say, "I give you permission to release (let go or exhale) those thoughts." Explain letting go is like deflating a balloon or tire. Children often unconsciously hang on to negative thoughts because they mistakenly feel this may be a way of attempting to please their parents. They need your permission to let these thoughts go. It also allows your child to see how his own thoughts feed anxiety.

USING "I" MESSAGES

Using "I" messages teaches children how to express themselves effectively with others. They are typically more productive than "you" statements as they are less likely to be received by others as an attack or threat. As your child learns to listen to his symptoms of anxiety, it will be important for him to recognize how certain "I" statements give him energy (decreasing anxiety) while others may deplete it (increasing anxiety). Those that increase anxiety are more likely to send mixed signals or shut down communication. Choosing "I" messages that boost energy illustrates to your child how taking care of himself and communicating clearly go hand in hand.

"I" Messages That Boost Energy

"I" messages that are closest to your heart and how you truly feel tend to be more uplifting and free of anxiety. *I am, I love, I feel, I appreciate, I need*, and *I see*, whether said aloud or silently to yourself, leave you feeling open, lifted, or lighter. Therefore, rather than focus on what you think you *should* say, consider going with the "I" statements that feel closest to your sincere thoughts and feelings. Your true thoughts and feelings are the ones you experience in the absence of anxiety. After all, if you did not genuinely love your child you would not be experiencing worry and concern for his anxiety. To deliver "I" messages in this way you and your child need to practice attending to your body first (exhaling, stretching, pausing) before speaking to others. Simply by bringing yourself into the here and now (through acknowledging your body), you are able to speak from a place of truth to yourself and others.

If using an "I" message feels fake or uncomfortable to your child, then he may have a belief about himself worth releasing. For example, if your child says "I am confident" and he is clearly uncomfortable, he may unconsciously believe he is weak, insecure, or fearful. Encourage him to release these beliefs using one of the techniques in Chapter 11 and then once again have him state, "I am confident." Encourage him to notice the difference in the way it feels.

"I" Messages That Deflate Energy

"I" messages that may deplete you or your child's energy are: *I can't, I don't know, I try, I'm tired, I'm busy, I am sick of,* or *I have had enough*. When you say these things aloud, notice the quality of energy that returns to you. Children sense and feel the difference between when you speak from your heart and when you speak from a place of reaction to your thoughts and fears. By paying attention to your own energy you will begin to pause to acknowledge yourself and your truth and then speak in ways that are mutually beneficial to you and your child.

"I" Messages Can Replace Blame

"I" messages focus on what you experience, rather than laying blame on someone else for making you feel or act in a certain way. Blame is similar to shame. It holds you back from experiencing your feelings, which are the gateway to opening up your child's heart and mind.

"I" statements maintain respectful means for communicating. Statements delivered with sarcasm, anger, or negative nonverbal signals like a clenched jaw or tightly crossed arms are reactions that demonstrate someone is controlling feelings rather than experiencing them. When children witness actions from truth they learn how to step into the authenticity of who they are. Truth is the experience of your emotions in flow. If your emotions are not flowing it is likely that you or your child may be caught in a web of untruths that for many of us shows up as fear. Love is truth. Teach your children to make decisions from a state of love rather than from a place of fear (e.g., What if).

REFLECTIVE LISTENING

Reflective listening occurs when a person acts as a sort of mirror for another, reflecting back what they observe, with just a bit of interpretation. This type of listening is actually the basis of most forms of psychotherapy, and recent research indicates that it can foster the development of new brain structures that mitigate depression and anxiety. Reflective listening validates the other person's experience and communicates empathy and understanding. It also opens the door for more and deeper communication, which is especially important with a child experiencing anxiety. Therefore, if your child says in a trembling voice, "I don't want to go to school today," you might say, "I see you are anxious about school. Is it because of your math test?"

ADDITIONAL WAYS TO OPEN COMMUNICATION

Parents can shut down opportunities to communicate with their child without realizing it. When it comes to raising children, quality is more important than quantity. Let's face it, a long extensive conversation is pretty rare in the parent-child relationship. To increase communication, avoid asking only yes or no questions such as, "Are you hungry?" or "Did you have a good day?" Instead, ask open-ended questions like, "What was lunch like today? Who did you sit with?" Be patient and watch for certain times of the day when your child may be more open to having a conversation. Directly after school may work for you, but not your child. Sitting in silence is okay, too—remember that nonverbal communication works as well. Try not to talk on the phone when you're riding in the car with your child. Your presence speaks volumes!

> The practice of reflective listening helps both you and your child. You get to experience and reinforce the discipline of attending to the moment, and your child gets to feel heard and valued. The key is to listen without judgment and refrain from trying to fix, evaluate, or give unsolicited advice about what your child is saying.

Reframing

Your language, including the words, tone of voice, and expression you use, has the power to stimulate or lessen anxiety in yourself and others. Learning how to reframe your child's language is an essential tool for toning down stress and creating the possibility for higher thinking and inner growth. To reframe something means to say it in another way. Positive statements send the nervous system messages of calm, relaxation, improved blood flow, and ease. Children and adolescents who are stressed or anxious tend to see things in a negative light. This is typically heard through their choice of words and seen through their irritability, or at times their disrespectful behavior. Anxious kids say things like "I can't" or "it won't work." Reframe this by using phrases like "I look forward to figuring this out," or "This is difficult but I know it will work out." You may also encourage your child to reframe his thoughts himself by asking a question: "What evidence do you have that it won't work out?" This challenges negative thinking, and helps your child to see how irrational thinking can contribute to anxiety.

Teaching Kids How to Feel

Teaching children about their facial expressions and what they mean (happy, mad, sad) is how young children are taught about their feelings. However, as children get older, solely relating their emotions to what occurs on the outside may confuse feelings with actions. For example, if you ask your child what anger *feels* like, she might demonstrate yelling or put her hands on her hips and point her finger. This is an opportunity to teach her that feeling is not an action, but rather an inner experience of your bodily sensations. Progressive muscle relaxation is a way to demonstrate these sensations. Tell your child to squeeze her fists tightly and then release. This is what sensation feels like when it is flowing. Notice when you clench your fists or face you stop breathing. When you release your fists you automatically begin to exhale. Energy is released and as this occurs sensations begin to arise in your body. These sensations are your emotions (which are vibrational frequencies) moving. As a result of this moving you feel better. Increasing sensations (e.g., through physical exercise, breathing, etc.) provides relief from emotions like fear, worry, and anger that have been building up. It also circulates oxygen, glucose, and uplifting neurotransmitters such as dopamine, oxytocin, and serotonin. Breathing from your lower belly (expanding out on inhale, and contracting in on exhale) works in the same way. This increased circulation renews your child's perception, allowing him to feel first rather than act first and skip feeling. Actions from experiencing acknowledged feelings tend to be driven from love and compassion, while actions from nonfeeling or ignored feelings are more likely to be triggered from fear and control. Here are ways you can encourage feeling:

O **Direct attention to your body.** Body awareness is the first step in feeling your emotions. Close your eyes and turn your attention to your body. Parents can help their children by encouraging them to close their eyes and think about each body part. Body parts with the most nerve endings such as your nose, fingertips, and face are often easier to tune in to.

O **Notice your sensations.** Sensations are experienced through your senses (touch, sight, hearing, taste, and smell). Some sensations are tingly, like having butterflies in your stomach, while others are dull. Anger, sadness, or guilt tend to be heavy with minimal movement while joy or appreciation are often light with lots of movement.

It's a Family Affair

Anxiety tends to cluster in families. This means your child can be affected by someone in the family who lives with anxiety, or your child's symptoms can have an effect on the family. It will be important for you and your partner (or your child's other biological parent) to look into the possibility that traits of anxiety have been traced through your family. Just like you can inherit eye color, families can also pass down mental characteristics. Research has shown us that Attention Deficit Hyperactivity Disorder, anxiety, and depression can run in families. This knowledge is helpful for the person who is exhibiting signs of anxiety, and any professionals who are supporting you.

If you suspect that there are family patterns that point to anxiety, gently explore them with your family members. Be aware of any chemical abuse or other addictive behaviors in your family, as these can be a coping mechanism for anxiety and depression.

Create a Support Team

Connecting and receiving support from others is essential to the human experience. Parenting is one of the most challenging jobs you will ever have. Some parents are fortunate to have built-in support from the start, meaning that they feel connected to their child's teachers and school staff, other parents, babysitter, neighbors, family, and the child's doctor. Others may have to work harder at developing relationships with others, or it may vary year to year. If you feel unsupported by the individuals whom you expect to support you, this may be a sign to get some help yourself. Talking with a therapist or counselor can be extremely helpful. Your willingness to look into and accept help can make a world of difference.

MEDICAL RESOURCES

Your child's medical team can be comprised of your child's doctor or nurse practitioner, and if necessary a psychiatrist. Alternative care providers like chiropractors, acupuncturists, nutritionists, or homeopaths can also be considered part of the medical team. Each team has its own unique set of players, and what works for one family might not look exactly the same for another.

SPIRITUAL RESOURCES

A place of worship may be a source of support and encouragement for both you and your child. Spirituality helps your child view herself as being much more than her accomplishments. Look for spiritual resources that restore your child's faith in her capabilities, offer love, respect, understanding, and compassion. Some places of worship offer counseling that you can accept if it feels right. Be aware that the spiritual community does not always view mental health issues in the same way that the medical system does. You may need to seek support if the two appear to be in conflict.

COMMUNITY RESOURCES AND SCHOOL

Community resources include community education, after-school programs, park and recreation programs, libraries, and even local businesses. If your child is uneasy about leaving home, but old enough to do so safely, you might consider working with a local shop owner to help your child in expanding her range. Perhaps your child could call you from the store or restaurant, or you could prepay for a treat she can collect when she arrives. Dance, music, theater, gymnastics, and martial arts can also provide great opportunities to practice social skills, build mastery, and learn self-reliance.

Connect to Truth

Being truthful requires tact and some self-awareness. Children experiencing anxiety can demand excessive time and attention, causing frustration and resentment to parents. Though you may need to express your feelings in order to set limits and help your child modify his behavior, remember to avoid shame or blame, because this will only magnify your child's worry and anxiety. Expressing the attitude that "we are all in this together" can help minimize the possibility that your child will internalize blame for expressing his feelings in the way that he does.

AGE APPROPRIATENESS

Explaining anxiety to your child will depend on developmentally appropriate terms and comparisons. Children tend to understand things better through real-life examples. Younger children need clear, concrete descriptions, and may respond to a "story" about another child with similar experiences. Older children do well if they are able to ask you questions based on their fears or worries. Doctors and therapists are trained to give facts in a way that is geared toward a child's level. A natural time to mention worries and fears is during your child's annual well visit or checkup. Telling your doctor about how your child is managing stress is no different than updating how well your child is eating and sleeping. The more you discuss it openly and honestly, the less uncomfortable it will be.

Dr. Paul Foxman, the director of the Center for Anxiety Disorders recommends a self-help program called the LifeSkills program (*http://chaange.com*) as a resource for children and adolescents diagnosed with an anxiety disorder. The program is designed to increase the ability to cope with stress, build confidence, and utilize social skills.

EFFECTS ON SIBLINGS

It's common for siblings of children receiving attention and care to feel jealous of the amount of time and energy spent by parents on their sibling. They may feel their sibling is favored and receiving special treatment they themselves are not entitled to. Siblings may also begin to withdraw from the family, perhaps by spending more time at a friend's house than at home. If you suspect this is happening, considering including the siblings in family therapy so they can have a voice in family discussions. Therapy can also provide an opportunity for siblings to learn strategies for coping and releasing strategies themselves. In addition, you may want to consider spending time with each of your children alone.

Effects on Partnerships and Marriage

Research shows an increased percentage of marital dissatisfaction in families with children who experience emotional setbacks. Because parents have varying levels of distress tolerance and coping, individual differences can be magnified when a couple is under stress. For example, an introverted spouse may become even more withdrawn when under stress, leading the other parent to feel unsupported or neglected.

It's important that you and your partner respect each other's process. Not everyone grows and learns at the same rate. One parent may be ready to jump in and take on new skills and strategies, while the other may need more time to digest and absorb the material. Parents who choose to focus on themselves rather than the other partner's faults or approaches will be able to move through the process with their child with more ease. As always, it is important to recognize each other's efforts and strengths.

Any time a family member receives a mental health diagnosis there is a natural sense of grief and loss that occurs. Some parents may experience a sort of "kicked in the gut" feeling, others may be sad and withdrawn, and still others feel angry with themselves, the child, the situation, or God. Research on the grieving process indicates that parents may have any or all of these reactions and may alternate between emotional states. Regarding your marriage, the most important factors are that you are able to communicate with each other about what you are experiencing individually and as a couple, and that you allow each other the space and time to process whatever feelings you experience in response to your child's health challenge.

Parenting Style

Since your child may be experiencing self-doubt, fear, and insecurity, your style of parenting is an important part of building self-esteem. Conscious parents strike a balance between being clear and consistent with communication and rules while allowing some freedom and flexibility. In other words, some rules are negotiable while others are not. Mistakes are often seen as opportunities to learn and children and adolescents are permitted to have a voice as long as it is delivered with respect. Because the child is given some power to make decisions but has consistent parental input, conscious parenting tends to foster self-reliance and self-regulation. Children also learn skills such as cooperation, communication, respect, and to honor individual and family values and differences.

STANDING TOGETHER

Because children experiencing anxiety often view things as out of control, it is especially important that parents be on the same page regarding how the symptoms are handled, whether or not they live under the same roof. Although it is typical for parents to differ in their approaches to childrearing, you can create a unified front by ensuring consistency in the following elements of family life:

O Keep negative or concerned conversations about your child or the other parent in private. Even if your child can't hear you, he can pick up on your tone.

O Agree to provide time for your child to exercise, extra time to get ready (rushing increases anxiety), and to monitor foods that exacerbate symptoms (sugar, caffeine).

O Let your child know ahead of time about changes in the schedule, what to expect for the week, and details such as who will pick them up from school.

○ Allow your parenting partner time for self-care and fun. Encourage each other to exercise, take a break, and get support when needed. Anxiety can be contagious and children often imitate what they learn.

Important Points to Consider

Your home should be a supportive environment for your child with anxiety. Because anxiety can often be contagious, meaning that your child will feed off your worries, it is critical that you try to foster a positive and open environment at home. Practice open communication with your child and help her to express herself so she can reduce her anxiety. Keep these important points in mind as you try to build the right home environment for your child:

○ Take advantage of every opportunity to communicate with your child. Be ready to talk when she is—and learn not to push it when she isn't.

○ Encourage your child to use "I" messages to reinforce the idea that she can control the way she feels about a situation.

○ Teach your child how to feel and experience her emotions and to release the negative ones that may be adding to her anxiety.

○ Anxiety affects the entire family. Make sure you communicate with the whole family about your child's symptoms and treatment plan.

○ Take time for yourself and your partner to connect. Having a child with anxiety can be hard on parents; make your relationship a priority as well.

CHAPTER 8

Parenting and Anxiety

Dealing with anxiety is all about letting go of expectations and pre-conceived notions, not only of your child, but also of how you might have expected parenting to be. Parenting often begins with a dream, compiled from illusions and greeting card images. Little did you know at that time that every birth brings a journey of ebb and flow. Picture a beautiful maple tree in the fall, losing its leaves as it prepares for the winds and storms of winter. To be strong and withstand the dark days as well as the light, it must first let go. Once it loses its leaves, it has less to carry and hold on to. It is no longer burdened, able to stabilize its roots into the ground, and bend its now flexible branches. Be the tree, let go, and know the lessons you experience are gifts received.

The Parent's Role

You are a role model for your children, and your fears about your own life or theirs will have an effect on your child's confidence and self-esteem. Her relationship with you and her imitation of your choices and behavior will influence her decisions about what life looks like, how she feels about herself in the world, and how capable she believes she is to manage that world. Letting your child see you experience some mild to moderate anxiety and resolving it effectively will be beneficial. Feelings of fear and anxiety are inevitable, and by watching you deal with it, your child will know that she, too, can meet difficulties in life head-on. However, if your fears for your child seem to create chaos or conflict, your child will perceive her own anxious moments this way as well. The message your child hears is, "I do not trust you to care for yourself or think you will make good decisions, so I must worry," and the child can then more easily internalize beliefs such as "I can't" or "I shouldn't."

Seeing Choices as Tools

You are a crucial element in your child's day-to-day functioning. The choices you make have the ability to stimulate or diffuse anxiety in the home. If you divorce, separate, start a new job, move, act abusively, try to be a perfect parent, use drugs or alcohol, or stress performance over experience, you are shaping your child. You are also shaping your child by exercising to keep fit, getting together with friends, taking a class to feed your own soul, or sitting down to relax and read a book for enjoyment. Even the rules you make in the house have the power to create anxiety or reduce it. For example, if the rule is "you must get an A in school because you are smart enough to do it" and there is a consequence for not making the grade, your child may be anxious about his performance. That might actually decrease your child's ability to concentrate and cause what the child is most afraid of: an inability to remember what he studied, and your consequent disappointment. If the rule is "you must do chores when you get home from school, and then do your homework before you can go out to play" and your child never finishes before dinner, your child may get frustrated and angry. Because your child loves you and wants to be seen as good, he may internalize his anger, and instead you will see an irritable, anxious, or depressed child.

Thriving Parents Equal Thriving Children

Since you are the cornerstone for your children's emotional and social development, your capacity to understand them will be a gift to them as they grow. This is also true when you show compassion for, and know how to interpret, their needs. Those qualities are crucial building blocks in your children's self-concept, ability to cope, and school readiness.

YOUR BEHAVIOR IS IMPORTANT

A group of American and German researchers studied 1,000 adolescent subjects, fourteen to seventeen years old, mostly middle class and attending school, and they found that more than genetics plays a part in a child developing an anxiety. Children who had parents with social phobia, depression, other anxiety disorders, who abused alcohol, or were overprotective or distant were at a significantly increased risk of developing social phobias. Other researchers concur that social fears may be learned, at least in part, from parents who are shy and withdrawn. However, genetic behavior is not a life sentence.

Many parents are turning to mindful-based programs and practices as a way to move through their own challenges with anxiety. The research on the benefits of mindfulness is abundant and continues to grow with concrete evidence for improving health, relationships, and emotional well-being. One study of "fifth-grade girls who did a ten-week program of yoga and other mindfulness practices were more satisfied with their bodies and less preoccupied with weight." ("The Science of Mindfulness," Dr. Daniel J. Siegel, Sept 7, 2010, *www.mindful .org/the-science-of-mindfulness*)

All it takes is one family member to become aware, open, and willing to try new behaviors to make long-lasting change. Science has proven that human beings have the ability to change their own DNA simply through modifying thoughts and behaviors. You really are that powerful.

PARENTING TRIGGERS

Parenting children through emotional ups and downs can trigger feelings and behaviors embedded in your memory. Triggers are memories or experiences that are revisited when you experience certain thoughts, feelings, sounds, or sights. Some triggers can be helpful, such as seeing your child's backpack may remind you to ask if she has homework. Other triggers, such as watching the clock or hearing siblings argue, may trigger behaviors in you that generate tension in the household.

Supporting your child through anxiety requires you to make a choice to pay attention to possible triggers that may be causing you to engage in counterproductive behaviors. Try to identify one or two triggers that quickly come to mind. In the beginning, choose triggers that are simple to work with. Over the next few days, begin to pay attention to the feelings you may be pushing away when you come across that trigger, perhaps a feeling of helplessness, hurt, anger, or fear. Notice the emotion, and see if you can allow yourself to receive even ten seconds of that feeling before responding to your child's behavior. Observe how just ten seconds of feeling what is behind the trigger alters the course you may take. Instead of yelling, you may speak firmly and respectfully to your child. Or instead of speaking at all, you may remove yourself to a private area where you can focus on your breathing.

THRIVING CONSCIOUS PARENTS

Thriving conscious parents are open, disciplined, and yet flexible. They allow themselves to be vulnerable, as they realize the experience of their emotions offers them sustainable energy, insight, connection, and growth. They not only seek help when needed, but are able to accept and receive it. Their connection to the moment allows them to sort out the tools and strategies that work well for them and their family. They believe in themselves, respect the journey of their child, and trust their own inner guidance. They recognize the beliefs, thoughts, and habits that hold them back. They take small steps as they create manageable goals for themselves and others. They take time for themselves, keep their passions alive, and surround themselves with healthy friendships and support. Conscious parents seek a path of contentment, are willing to shed what no longer serves them, hug their child on a regular basis, savor moments that offer connection, and remember to say, "I love you."

TIPS FOR CONSCIOUS PARENTS

Conscious parents believe that taking care of themselves will help them become better able to care for and guide their children. It is difficult to teach children what you have not experienced yourself. While you are juggling schedules, jobs, and household tasks, know that just by incorporating deep breathing into your life you are taking care of yourself. Create a habit of taking three deep breaths three times a day. This will decrease the chances that you will absorb the your child's fears while increasing your ability to apply the following guidelines.

- **Keep the boundaries between parenting and friendship clear.** Don't treat your child as your confidant. When children and adolescents feel as if they have to carry a parent's concerns and frustrations, this increases anxiety. Single parents may feel burdened by having to manage the emotional, physical, and intellectual well-being of their children on their own. Instead, find supportive resources such as a counselor, church group, support group, exercise class, friend, or family member you can speak to privately. Watch your behavior for signs of venting, as this is also something that exacerbates anxiety in yourself and children.

- **Allow your child to learn personal management.** This includes how to dress appropriately, remember his backpack, or how to handle arguments with siblings or friends. Let your kids discover how to be responsible to and for each other.

- **Allow your child to explore friendships.** Unless your child is in danger, being bullied, or taken advantage of, let him make decisions about whom he would like to play with. It is tempting to want to steer children in a certain direction or to want them to play with children you know. However, childhood is a time to learn about differences in individuals, relationships, and communication styles. Later, when your child is able to sort out on his own positive from negative influences, you will be able to see the benefits from the foundation you provided.

○ **Give your child the opportunity to show he can be successful.** This is especially important, even if he tried an activity before and it did not go well. Treat each moment, each day, as new. Know that your child is growing and changing daily; to base every decision on his past experiences and yours would negate the growth that is happening.

○ **If your child is afraid to go somewhere or try something new, gently encourage him or suggest small increments of engaging in the feared situation.** If he is afraid to sleep in his own bed, but you want him out of yours, begin by setting up an air mattress at the end of your bed. Each day, move it slightly. First move the mattress toward the door, and after a night or two of success there, move it into the hallway, and eventually into your child's room.

○ **There is no perfect balance.** There will naturally be times you and your child are more stressed than others. Notice if you strive for perfect balance in your life. This is an unrealistic expectation (often driven by anxiety) that requires a lot of energy to keep up. You are better off embracing that life is a journey of ebb and flow. To do this, focus on the flow of your breath (inhale, exhale) rather than attempting to control what is happening in your life.

Overprotective Parenting

Consider the following scenario: "Did you call Jimmy to play? Oh, okay, what time did you say you would be there? Don't forget to take your jacket just in case the weather turns cold, and don't forget to look both ways when you cross our street, and remember to say thank you to Mrs. Michael for inviting you, and if she offers you something to eat, remember to chew with your mouth closed, keep your elbows off the table, and say thank you when you are done. And, oh, don't forget to call me before you leave so I know you are on your way and can look for you as you make your way across the street."

Overparenting or being overprotective tends to have very negative consequences. The message your child will hear is, "I have to worry about you so much because you are not competent to deal with things on your own. You need my supervision and decision-making or this will end badly." Your child may feel angry and insulted by what seems like a put-down. Alternately, a child may simply quit trying because she feels she has no control in the world. Overparenting becomes the opposite of what a parent's most important job is: to encourage autonomy and foster a healthy self-concept.

Fostering dependency in your child can inhibit his attempts to learn to do things by himself. When a child has the view that he is incompetent without help from others, he can become discouraged and see himself as stuck.

WHAT THE DOCTORS SAY

Harvard psychologist Jerome Kagan, in researching temperament, has shown that parents hovering and protecting them from stressful experiences can often cause anxiety in children. He found that infants who were born "overexcitable" tended to cope better with life and had a more positive outlook if their parents gave them freedom to do, think, and make mistakes on their own.

Michael Liebowitz, professor of clinical psychiatry at Columbia University and former director of the Anxiety Disorders Clinic at New York State Psychiatric Institute, believes parents can have well-adjusted children if they take the time to gently encourage their children to try new things, even if they are scared, so they can learn that nothing bad will happen. "They need gradual exposure to find that the world is not dangerous. Having overprotective parents is a risk factor for anxiety disorders because children do not have opportunities to master their innate shyness and become more comfortable in the world."

The general consensus is that when children are overprotected they never learn to modify or reshape the connections in their brain. Allow your child to change her perceptions, by continuous modification of what is feared, so the anxiety does not become the pattern of her life.

When Parents Are Depressed

A good therapist understands that when a child is struggling or having trouble with daily life, you will often find at least one parent who is depressed. Psychologists have also learned that even though the parents come to therapy and identify the child as the source of their distress, it is often more likely that the child has been reacting to the parent's depression.

Depression may be the cause of anxiety, even if you don't feel depressed. Sometimes it shows up feeling numb or withdrawn. Stephen Cope, MSW, the founder and former Director of the Kripalu Institute for Extraordinary Living, observes that, "Depression manifests as our inability to be present for the experience of life."

HOW YOUR STRESS AFFECTS YOUR CHILD

It is easy to forget that your children have ears. Even if they are not in the room, that does not mean they are not listening. When children hear you argue or yell, they may internalize your experience and make it their own. This type of response may cause depression, anxiety, or mistrust in people and relationships. This is unlikely to occur immediately, but over time a child internalizes these feelings. Children of stressed parents feel the need to read their parents' moods and tone of voice as a way to judge how safe it is to be around them or to ask for what they need. This type of pattern teaches children to be preoccupied with fear and to instinctively want to control the future. As a result, assertiveness and the ability to handle confrontation may become underdeveloped.

People who are depressed often have counterproductive posture and breathing patterns. Gentle yoga classes that encourage correct posture and the proper way to take a long inhale and exhale can help lift mood. Any exercise will help to boost mood, along with eating less sugar and incorporating healthy fats and omega-3–enriched foods.

Part of managing your stress is a willingness to watch your own behaviors. How do you handle stress? Do you unconsciously reach for food, a cigarette, a beer or glass of wine, or use foul language when you are under pressure? Or do you breathe, take a walk, read, spend time alone, exercise, think loving thoughts, go to bed early, eat healthy foods, take a bath, connect to people, ask for help, say "no" when necessary, allow yourself to cry, or do something you love? Your behavior is an example to your children, no matter what their age.

How Is Your Marriage?

The state of your marriage can have a deep and lasting effect on your children. Arguments and issues to resolve are normal, and in fact can teach your child how to handle conflict appropriately as she grows. However, when yelling has no resolution, when you call each other names, and when everyone walks away hurt, sad, or angry, negative connections are made. You and your spouse or parenting partner are role models for what your child will come to expect from relationships, so take a moment to ask yourself what you are really modeling. This may require you and your partner to take some time together to revisit what you value, engage in active listening, or to connect to the hobbies and interests that brought you together in the first place.

QUESTIONS TO HELP YOU BECOME SELF-AWARE

Because of the value modeling has on the growth of your children, your relationship with your significant other will certainly be something you want to think about and possibly improve. You have the ability to influence your child's anxiety for the better through your own self-awareness. Self-awareness allows you to be open and grow in an emotional environment of kindness and compassion.

Letting go of anxiety and interrupting the cycles is an internal journey. It's never too late to become mindful. Mindful approaches are timeless and not only decrease anxiety but also improve memory, health, relationships, and overall satisfaction with life. It's not uncommon to discover these amazing benefits while offering support and care to a loved one.

After taking three long deep breaths, reflect on the following questions. Ask yourself:

O Are you willing and ready to forgive and be forgiven?

O Are you willing and ready to let go of past arguments?

O Are you willing and ready to treat each day as new?

O Are you willing and ready to truly listen without distractions or interruptions?

O Are you willing and ready to honor the wounds of the past as teachable moments?

O Are you willing and ready to accept your human nature, to make mistakes safe, and to keep your expectations of each other realistic?

O Are you willing and ready to see the good rather than focusing on the not-so-good in each other?

O Are you willing and ready to take responsibility, to own your own anxiety, and to give self-love strategies a fair chance?

- Are you willing and ready to accept that your needs, wants, desires, and dreams are equally important?

- Are you willing and ready to thrive, rather than survive, during your parenting journey?

In this sacred partnership of parents, together you are one. Whether you are living together or not, you both impact the experiences of your child. Your children serve as reflections of your state of mind. You have the power to influence these reflections. It is never too late. Focus on the times you do this well rather than the times you let yourself and others down. This will build resiliency and help you develop your ability to be and live peacefully.

Separation, Divorce, and Blended Families

There is as much conflicting evidence about the effects of separation and divorce on children as there are studies. There are books that say children of divorce or separated parents will suffer more from depression and anxiety, have lower self-esteem, and tend to tolerate or exhibit more abuse and neglect in their own relationships. There are also books that tell you that staying together in a high-conflict marriage will cause exactly the same issues. Some researchers have said that low-conflict marriages where the parents just do not love each other anymore and divorce anyway will cause the most anxiety and depression for a child. Research on blended families has also yielded lots of conflicting evidence.

Researchers have found that adolescents find it the most difficult to adjust to a blended family arrangement. Although young children want to engage with a stepparent if that parent is seen as warm, engaging, and available, they still have considerable anxiety over how to be loyal to their own absent parent. Adolescents, because of their age, developing sexuality, and establishing autonomy, can find the presence of a stranger in the house disruptive and anxiety-provoking.

YOUR CHILD'S AGE MAKES A DIFFERENCE

If your child is in preschool, research confirms he will miss the parent who has moved out of the home and have a greater need for safety and security. He might, because of his anxiety and fears, regress in his most recent developmental accomplishment. He might have difficulty sleeping, be fearful, irritable, aggressive, demanding, or depressed and withdrawn. Children ages five to eight can be more self-blaming and verbal about their sadness, be scared you will find another family to love instead, and have difficulty understanding what "permanent" means. They may be forgetful, seem to lose time, or seem to be in a dream state. Children ages nine through adolescence tend to be more vocal, angry, resentful, blaming, and often act out in a more hostile way.

If your child persistently displays behaviors such as withdrawal, self-harm, anger, depression, and/or anxiety because you have divorced, separated, or blended your family with another, it is important to look into therapy.

According to Jane Nelson, the author of *Positive Discipline for Blended Families*, "Young children are especially sensitive to non-verbal messages adults send them. They can 'read' energy long before they can speak words. And when an adult's words and non-verbal messages don't match, they instinctively trust the non-verbal part."

CONSCIOUS PARENTING TIPS FOR DIVORCED AND BLENDED FAMILIES

To lessen the anxiety your child will feel during separation and divorce, here are some key points to remember: First, let your child be a child. The best you can do for him right now is keep what happens between you and your partner private, and do not put him in a position of parenting you or being your emotional caretaker. Some kids may attempt to do this even when you try to prevent it. They are merely trying to have some sense of control over their situation. Give them some other way of having control, like choosing when they do their homework—either after school or after dinner. Maybe you can let them choose how many books they want you to read them before bed, or allow them to decide which chores they feel they would be best at, instead of telling them which ones they will do.

To lessen a child's anxiety, no matter what age, it is very important during a time of change to keep your promises, be consistent, and have a routine. While blending families together, the most important element of the process is communication. That means you communicate to your children and allow them to communicate to you. Having a family meeting once a week is an excellent start.

Keep in mind that the new stepparents, and possibly stepsiblings, are *your* choice, not necessarily your child's. It is important to have compassion for how this might feel for them and realize that it can take years to work out. That does not mean your kids are being difficult, or that something is wrong with your family. Lastly, to reduce both anxiety and conflict, it is best to let the biological parent remain primarily responsible for control and discipline of their own children until the children feel they have developed a strong bond with the stepparent. This often means after a few years, not after weeks or months. This rule is especially important for adolescents, who may already be struggling with authority and independence issues.

Important Points to Consider

You can have a positive impact on your child's anxiety simply by making positive choices for yourself. You are the role model for how your child will handle his emotions and anxiety in life, so choose right from the beginning to be a good one. If you find you are depressed or overprotective, you need to seek help so that you do not negatively impact your child and add to his anxiety. Here are some other key things to keep in mind:

- As a parent, your child will look to you as a gauge for how he forms his perceptions about acting and being in his own life. If you are anxious, stressed, or depressed, your child will most likely be as well.

- When adjustments are going to occur for your child that are out of his control, help him feel he is being taken into account by communicating with compassion and by being your best self. This will allow him to feel safe as he is struggling to navigate through the change.

- Being your best self means taking an inventory of your ability to live with stress, your emotional life, and your marriage. Looking for ways to find balance in these areas benefits both you and your child.

CHAPTER 9

Conscious Parenting Pointers

One of the greatest challenges all parents face is learning how to respond to household tension. Although you can't control or fix how your child responds to the demands and stresses placed upon her, you can influence them. Keep in mind that there are no perfect parents and it is normal to go through ups and downs. But there are ways that you can use conscious parenting techniques to reduce the anxiety your child feels during these times.

Consistency and Follow-Through

To a child with anxiety, missing the ball in a soccer game or having a homework assignment due at school can be opportunities for disaster and the final proving ground for how ineffective she feels in her life. Providing stability, security, and consistency can increase your child's sense of self-worth and ease negative thoughts. When life feels tenuous and out of control, having clear rules, consequences, and order are best.

CONSISTENCY

Being reliable and predictable is potent medicine for an anxious child. Children need to know what and whom they can count on. This is not to say spontaneity won't be of value to your child. However, on a day-to-day basis, an organized lifestyle with fairly predictable routines is best. Routines are like anchors: They minimize worry. Children don't have to figure out daily when dinner will be served, when to do homework, and what time you will be home. Busy families can post calendars on refrigerators or in an area that children see every day, with everyone's schedule spelled out.

To foster consistency, the rules you make for the household need to remain constant until you have a family meeting or other opportunity to sit down with your child and identify the new expectation and related consequence. Because children with anxiety can become overwhelmed easily, anticipating and averting unnecessary triggers is helpful. With that in mind, it might be important to set a specific time to do homework, have a set time for meals, plan and organize projects for school with a timeline, and consistently reward your child if he sets a goal and accomplishes it. For children with anxiety, consistency can equal stability. When you think about how to bring consistency into your family, you can also ask, "What can we implement to make life feel more stable?"

It is best to have clear rules early on, with you making the decision about what is best, while honoring your child's desires and changing abilities. As children grow older, you can offer small choices and see how they do with them, limiting their choices to two specific options at first. If they struggle too much with a choice, you'll know you took this step too early. That's fine. Stop for now and try again in six months.

FOLLOW-THROUGH

Like consistency, follow-through for children can translate to security and trust. Creating an environment at home that optimizes your child's ability to count on you doing what you told her you would do, even if it means a consequence for her behavior, is important for anxiety reduction. The foundation parents instill with follow-through in the home can increase a child's ability to have trust, and decrease worry in relationships outside the home.

> When parents give choices, the child then has to make a decision. That is a big task for kids with anxiety who do not trust themselves. They end up agitated out of a sense of fear, seem to be procrastinating when they are actually unable to make a choice, and they then feel worse about themselves. It is therefore best to limit choices to two or three and to avoid language such as "go figure it out yourself."

This is also true for building an environment where children feel they can work through a hurtful communication with a parent or sibling and where they feel accepted exactly as they are. Telling your child you care that she is struggling with anxiety is one thing; showing her by helping her succeed is how she will *know* you care. Follow-through also means keeping your commitments. A child experiencing anxiety already has enough questions about life and people, and when parents or caregivers do not keep their word or use threats to manage situations, the world is perceived as unstable and the parent loses credibility in a child's eyes.

Changing your mind, breaking a promise, or being arbitrary with siblings and rules gives a child mixed messages. Besides undermining trust and security, these events might create anger and resentments, not only between you and your child, but between the anxious child and her siblings as well.

Being Active and Proactive

Most children, especially when young, do not plan ahead for a situation that creates anxiety. That means your child will likely approach an issue in the same ineffective way time after time. Understandably, this can perpetuate a sense of failure and an inability to trust herself. If you know from experience that allowing your child to be in charge of herself in the morning creates havoc and anxiety, step in and offer support.

In addition, if you know that time and organizational skills are areas needed for growth, be proactive. Identify the source of stress and set up a plan to create opportunities for success without everyone having to go through the stress of failure first. For example, say your son is invited to a birthday party. He is especially excited because it means some of the boys at school like him enough to want him there. However, when you get there he freezes at the door, grabs your leg, and refuses to go inside. At first you gently encourage and coax. When that does not work, you plead. Finally, you scold him and shake him off of you with embarrassment and irritation as the other boys and moms watch. Walking away, you are frustrated and perplexed that an exciting, fun event turned into a disaster and feel terrible for how you left him.

This situation gives you and your son an opportunity to develop a plan, proactively, for the future. The next time a new situation comes up, you two can sit down the day before to discuss it. You can talk about how he feels about being invited, what the most fun parts of the party might be, what he thinks they might all do, what he might be nervous about, and what his greatest fears might be. You also might suggest that you do not mind staying for a few extra minutes until he is settled in with his friends, or picking him up early. Most kids will agree to go to a party if they know they have a way out of what they fear most, and when the scary part comes they often are having so much fun they do not want to leave after all.

Intentional Planning

At the heart of every well-constructed plan is a clear intention. Intentions come from inside, typically drawn from what you love and care about. For example, you may have the intention of creating opportunities for your child to experience her capability, worthiness, and strength. Before building your goals and the steps you will take to achieve them, focus on what it is you are looking for. Ask:

1. What is my intention? (To provide opportunities for my child to feel worthy.)

2. What do I hope to see as a result? How will I know if the plan works? What behaviors might I see? (My child will be able to complete a task without reassurance or direction.)

3. What is one goal that will help me move in this direction? (Delegate tasks that my child is capable of.)

4. What is one possible intervention to achieve this goal? (Stop hovering over my child, instead allowing her to learn from her own experiences.)

A 2003 study had participants write down five things they were grateful for, each week for a period of ten weeks. Results showed that when compared to people in control groups who wrote down their day's frustrations or simply listed the day's events, these participants were 25 percent happier, more optimistic about the future, and participated in one and a half hours more exercise per week than those in the control groups.

Patience Really Is a Virtue

There is no quick fix for anxiety sufferers. A large component of anxiety is fear-based and personal, so there is no "one size fits all" solution. What worked for another child and family may not work for yours. As a caregiver, it will not be uncommon to have some intense feelings yourself. A thoughtful approach with a plan may take longer to set in place and execute, but will probably be a lot more effective and helpful than any quick fix. Quick fixes sound easy and provoke an eagerness to have a "normal" life back. Avoid comparing your situation to others. You and your child's journey are unique and with patience you begin to see the lessons and skills that unfold from it.

WATCH AND ENCOURAGE

Be patient, even if it means a job will not be done completely or in a timely fashion, and allow your child to have the experience of doing it for himself. Some children need to feel their anxiety, without parental intervention. Learning how to respect and experience your emotions is a foundational practice for building a supportive home environment. Part of the development of internal motivation comes from feeling stress.

For example, say your daughter tells you she has a project due at school in three days. You have already helped a number of times with setting up a plan, establishing a timeline, and seeing her accomplish the project. Out of your own fear because of how projects have gone in the past, and the irritability it caused for both of you, you might want to jump right in and say, "Okay, let's get started; first, why don't you . . . ." Try instead, "I trust you have all the tools needed to do a great job with that. You did such a terrific job on the last one. Why don't you get started, and I'll be by after I do the dishes to check it out." When you go to see how far she has gotten, be patient with whatever situation you walk into. Encourage, but do not take over, even if it took her an hour to get her materials together. Ask what she has decided her next step should be and gently guide her if she is off track.

It can be a slow process, but it's necessary if you ever want her to be able to have a healthy sense of self-confidence and to work on her own. Being anxious about how long she is taking or initiating the well-intentioned rescue just sets you up to have to rescue her again next time. Your job as a parent is to help your child learn how to help herself.

PROCRASTINATION

It helps to realize that most children with anxiety do procrastinate. They can have a hard time thinking things through, and if they are stuck in a ritual or familiar process of self-doubt, they will not get very far with a task.

Procrastination is a form of self-sabotage; it blocks your child from feeling a sense of accomplishment. Children who procrastinate often feel stuck. Inside they may know they need to make changes but are unsure about what changes to make. Many times they hang on to what is familiar (procrastination) out of fear of feeling what is unfamiliar. As a parent it's important to encourage your child to slowly shift her ways. Perhaps encouraging her to start her homework thirty minutes rather than one hour earlier is more realistic.

Try not to take your child's procrastination personally. For example, notice if you feel disrespected, ignored, or challenged in any way. Procrastination may be a trigger for some parents, and typically what fuels this trigger is an underlying fear that your child will fail or that you have somehow failed as a parent. Once you allow yourself to own that truth and take a moment to feel your fear rather than react to it, you and your child can begin to go about making changes that work for everyone.

Remember that lectures, repeating commands, yelling, and interrupting fuel your child's anxiety. Less is more. Be clear about what you are asking for. For example, rather than saying, "Clean your room," instead say, "Make your bed, put away clean laundry, and bring dirty laundry downstairs." Keep the number of tasks low so your child can feel a sense of completion.

It is common to have strong feelings when your children are having difficulty, so talk with a friend, your spouse, or a therapist instead of directing frustration at yourself or your child.

Defuse Situations

According to recent research, the same regions of the brain become activated whether you are observing a specific gesture or expression or making it yourself. This means your facial expressions and hand gestures can have an impact on your child's brain. Think about the times when your child became upset because you waved your hand to move him away. Perhaps you did not say anything verbally; however, the gesture itself was enough to change the experience (the resulting brainwaves) of the other person. This indicates how important it is for parents to take full responsibility for their actions. It also indicates how the power of a smile, gaze, or similar gesture of love sends out positive, uplifting energy that can affect the brainwaves of both the sender and the receiver.

Part of being calm is to exude an air of knowing or confidence. Verbal statements like "I know you are upset, but I trust you can do this," or "I know this feels hard for you. You are strong though, I've seen it," can be calming and helpful. Your child needs to feel your confidence in her. She counts on you when her emotions are too big for her to handle and logic is lost to her. If your child is misbehaving, it is best not to argue or debate with her. Quietly remind her of the rules and consequences of her behavior and ask if she would like to engage in some calming behavior, or take the consequence. If your child chooses to use tools to de-escalate, praise her with confidence: "I knew you could do this. I am so proud of you," or, "Wow, look at you! I love your creativity and strength."

If your child has a meltdown, don't assume falling apart was her choice, because sometimes, just as with a tantrum, the anxiety is so big that she can't figure out how to get on top of it anymore. Follow up with your child after a struggle or meltdown. When she is calm, ask why it went too far, and use the information to discuss and understand how all experiences help us grow and prepare for the future. Most of all, don't be afraid of your child's feelings. They are just emotions, and with awareness they will pass.

Routine Is King

Regular patterns and routines tend to diminish anxiety and increase the supply of confidence and peace. Children or adults experiencing anxiety feel calmer in daily life when it is predictable, when they know what is expected of them, and they are on a schedule. It is best to set specific times for meals, playtime, homework, quiet time, and bedtime. However, while an established routine is beneficial, you will want to avoid rigidity so that your child can practice flexibility from time to time.

For example, help your child establish a bedtime routine. This means you do the same things in the same order and at the same time every night. For example, at 7:30 P.M. your child takes a bath, then brushes his teeth and combs his hair. By 8:00 P.M., he is in his bed and it is story time until 8:15 P.M. He then gets to choose to read for an additional fifteen minutes by himself, or chat with you about his day. Lights are out at 8:30 P.M. If you have a child who finds it difficult to fall asleep, quiet music, a story, or recorded relaxation exercise works well. Keep in mind that new routines can take several weeks to establish, so hang in there.

Co-Parenting

It is especially important, no matter if you are living together, blended, separated, or divorced from your child's other parent, that you engage in healthy conversations about parenting and managing your child's anxiety. Agreement concerning the child can give your child one less thing to be anxious about, and the consistency of your approaches gives your child the structure she needs. For example, bedtime schedules and routine need to be the same even if one parent is not at home for the evening. If you live separately and choose different routines, that is okay, but you still need consistency. Each house should have a particular routine your child can count on when she is at that house.

If you find that your partner is not following through on an agreement, it is best to let the other know without doing it in front of the children. Maybe a tap on the shoulder as you walk by, or a squeeze of the hand could be just the reminder your partner needs. It is best not to discuss frustrations or react angrily in front of a child with anxiety. The guilt and esteem issues she has already will only be complicated if she believes you are upset with each other because of her. You can be honest with your child and let her know that it is okay to disagree; how you resolve the issue is what is most important.

WHAT AFFECTS YOU

Be as honest as you can with yourself and your partner or co-parent about your own childhood and how it might be influencing you now as a parent. Rather than judge, criticize yourself, or feel guilt because you are struggling, be open about your issues so you can get support. For example, if you were taught that "good" children were seen and not heard and now you have a child who breaks down emotionally, you might react negatively, or even overreact to your child. If the co-parent knows this and your child starts to act up, he can take over and give support to both of you. It does not mean you are entitled not to grow in that area; it does mean, though, that your child's emotional health is important and you both recognize you still have work to do in that area. That is what collaborating is about.

BEING A BETTER PARENT

Try to create one voice when parenting and to openly listen to your co-parent. Listening does not mean you agree, it just means you respect that the other parent has a thought or opinion to share. In addition, watch what you say in front of your child. Talk over disagreements in private and make your home a safe haven.

Although it may be tempting at times to throw in the towel, it's important to model for your children that decisions made from reactivity in a state of high anxiety may lead to further problems. If you're experiencing conflict or struggles it's a good idea to seek help and to find ways to release your own emotions of anger, guilt, or shame before making any rash decisions.

HELP YOURSELF

You can find information on the web, at bookstores, the library, at your child's school, from your doctor, and through friends and family. Although there are hundreds of websites about anxiety, some are better and more complete than others are. If you go to a bookstore, look in the self-help section and the children's section for books on anxiety and mental health. When visiting your local library you can talk with a librarian or use the computerized catalog to find books, journals, recordings, and magazine articles. Finding a support group online or in your community is also a great asset. You need to know that you are normal, even when you are upset with your child with anxiety, and that will happen when you find others with similar journeys.

Transform Your Rules Into Empowerment Tools

Today, new research is giving parents an incentive for relinquishing the word "no" (unless, of course, it is used to keep your child safe, like preventing him from running into the road). This creates an opportunity for making over how you prepare and state your rules. Taking the time to remove your "nos" can truly make a difference in the way your child responds to both your written and verbal rules. Doing this means you will be transforming your rules into empowerment tools.

> Rules are important. However, follow-through is what distinguishes an effective rule from an ineffective one. Pulling your child aside rather than speaking to him in front of others is mindful, respectful, and effective.

To begin transforming your rules you must first review the purpose of them. For most parents the purpose is to create a safe, cooperative environment conducive to learning and living with each other. Rules often reflect family values such as respect, hard work, and/or cooperation. The research shows that focusing on what you value sends a signal to your body that it is safe. Information that is interpreted by the body and brain as safe is more likely to be received in a calm way. This insight provides incentive to parents and educators to watch how their rules are stated. Following are some steps that will help you shift gears from enforcement to empowerment:

1. **Change rules to values.** Renaming "rules" as "values" does two things: One, it prevents you from overusing the word no; and two,

values are nonthreatening to children and adolescents. Values promote a sense of belonging, connection, and inner strength. For example, if you were to write your rules on a whiteboard, rather than phrasing the rule as "No name calling," you could state it positively as "We value respect for self and others."

2. **Rather than state your rules, create them.** Rules are not random; they are set deliberately to create a context for certain behaviors, and restating them is done in response to a specific misdemeanor. On occasion you might take the time to sit with your child to discuss the rules, but usually it's in response to the rules being broken in some way. If your goal is to tone down stress in the family environment, it is a good idea for you and your child to create the rules together. To do this, you have to ask your child to tap into her imagination. You might ask, "If our family were being respectful to one another, what would that look like? How would we do it?" You and your child can then come up with a mental image and describe it to each other. You may even have your child draw a picture of it. This creative process of personalization helps her internalize and understand the values.

3. **Rather than enforce, embody.** To truly own something, you must embody it. Think about it: Why wouldn't you own and embrace self-respect, patience, individuality, and cooperation? To do this well, you must be willing to feel what you value.

Example of a Rule Makeover

Following is an example of a rule moving through the three steps of transformation. Notice the difference between the way it is stated at the top and at the bottom. Notice the difference in feeling, and think about how it may promote peace and harmony in your home.

O **Rule:** No phones at the table.

O **Value:** We value time to connect.

O **State:** No phones at the table.

- **Create:** How will we behave if we value this meal as time together? What does our behavior look like if we are connected?

- **Enforce:** You just lost your phone.

- **Embody:** I appreciate everyone putting away their phones for dinner.

Reframe Language

Your words are powerful, and new science suggests they can trigger a response in someone else's amygdala, the part of the brain that signals fight or flight to the body. Reframing language is worth exploring as it not only impacts the response of your own brain, but also that of your child.

To reframe your language, there are three words to be aware of: "should," "no," and "don't." *Should* is a word that implies your child is wrong. It sets her up for feeling bad before she can feel good. This is a counterproductive pattern that is unnecessary and makes life appear so much harder than it is. The word *no*, as already stated, triggers fear or acts as a signal to your child's brain and body that it is unsafe. Again, there are times you will have to use the word "no," but in most cases you will choose an alternative. The third word to reframe is *don't*. *Don't* is dangerous because it often points to behavior you do not want to see. For example, "Don't touch that." Particularly for small children, it is more beneficial to redirect them to the activity or appropriate behavior that you do wish to see. By changing your words, you can influence the neurocircuitry in your brain as well as your child's. This makes it more likely that you and your child will activate other parts of your brain that promote harmony. Here are some examples of how to reframe your language:

RATHER THAN:	REFRAME TO:
O You should pick up after yourself	O Please pick up your plates and trash
O Don't touch your sister's things	O Ask before you touch
O No whining	O Use a clear voice

Strengthening Your Right Brain

The human brain has two hemispheres, the right and left brain. The left brain tends to live in the past and in the future. It helps you remember to go to your doctor appointment, do your laundry, and pick up what you need for dinner. Your right brain helps you connect to the present moment through your consciousness and awareness. It is the part of you that promotes feeling before thinking. The right brain is strengthened through experiences that engage the senses and emotional self through activities that promote creativity, mindfulness, movement, meditation, sound, and prayer. Strengthening your right brain lowers your reactivity. It does this because the right brain lives predominately through the present moment (where anxiety does not exist). The present moment is where you and your child think the most clearly and are the most resilient to the pressures and fears around you.

Children with anxiety tend to have overdeveloped left brains, the hemisphere that lives in the past and the future. Teaching children tools for redirecting their right brain to the present moment will be essential to increasing their wisdom and ability about how they can decrease their own anxiety. It is helpful if you teach them how to think in pictures and utilize their imaginations. Remember, the body and mind do not know the difference between a real or imagined threat. They respond as if everything is happening right now. This is valuable information; if your child's body does not *know* the difference between a real and imagined threat, that means it cannot *identify* the difference between a real and imagined threat. Therefore, if your child imagines a calm and peaceful scene or image (sun, tree, ocean, mountains), then your child's body (and brain) acts as if that image is happening right now. The same thing occurs when your child hears an inspirational or heartfelt story. When used consciously you can engage and strengthen your child's right brain through storytelling and visualization.

Ample scientific evidence exists to prove that stretching and yawning can reduce stress and provide an emotional release in the body.

Keep in mind that if your child is exposed to fearful images or stories, or if he is constantly plugged into the television and/or computer, this weakens his capacity to utilize his built-in abilities to overcome anxiety and be in the present moment. However, by slowly incorporating choices that develop your right brain, you show your child how human beings are not fixed. You can learn, grow, and change at any age.

Important Things to Consider

How you parent has a big impact on your child's anxiety. Using conscious parenting techniques that focus on consistency and intentional planning will lessen the amount of anxiety your child feels. Of course there will still be situations that raise your child's anxiety and she will still try to avoid things that make her afraid, but with patience and self-awareness you can help ease her burdens. Keep the following ideas in mind:

- Have consistent rules, and follow through on those rules. This will provide a sense of reliability for your child.

- Routines are an anchor for children with anxiety. While some spontaneity may be okay occasionally, consistent routines will give your child a sense of safety.

- Patience is paramount. Your child's anxieties and repeating patterns of avoidance may get frustrating for you, but by being patient and supportive you empower your child to believe that she can accomplish her goals.

- Reframe your family rules to eliminate the traditional language that seeks obedience and compliance. Making your rules more empathetic and value-centric will help tone down the stress in your household and lower your child's anxiety.

CHAPTER 10

Disciplining Children with Anxiety

As a conscious parent you tend to take a nonjudgmental, empathetic approach to discipline, but that doesn't mean you don't set limits or ignore bad behaviors in your children. Disciplining children with anxiety, however, can be tricky, because parents may already feel as if they are on shaky ground. A child's self-esteem may appear frail and his threshold for stress low. Small steps are key with a child who has anxiety. Planning and preparing in small pieces allows your child to reap better results and achieve his goals without becoming overwhelmed. Often when a child takes on too much or disregards his responsibilities, things build and explode into perceived problems and roadblocks. This can lead to disrespectful behavior such as a bad attitude, talking back, or teasing others. Discipline is a tool, not a punishment. The intent of discipline is to build your child's ability to manage his life by permitting carefully guided natural, logical consequences to actions.

Self-Regulation over Self-Control

Self-regulation is the ability to calm yourself down when you are upset. Self-control, on the other hand, may be misconstrued by your child as needing to control (stop) his feelings. This sends conflicting messages about how to live with stress and anxiety. When you allow the energy of your emotions to travel through your body instead of trying to force them down, you feel better, are able to think more clearly, and can respond in ways that not only benefit you but also the individuals around you. Explain to your child that stopping or suppressing feelings is like building an internal traffic jam. It creates inner conflict and sends mixed signals to the nervous system. On the other hand, self-regulation uses self-awareness as a way to move through that traffic. For example, when you cross a street you have to judge the situation by noticing the sounds and sights, and decide whether danger is present. You have to rely on your sense of awareness of the external situation and how your sense of self-awareness interacts with it to get to the other side of the road safely and, hopefully, without triggering fear and anxiety.

It is difficult for a young child to understand the difference between a thought and a feeling. Here is a way you might explain the difference: "A thought is something that happens in your head, like all of a sudden when you see your toothbrush and you think, 'Oh, Mommy said to brush my teeth!' A feeling is something that might happen in your stomach or heart, like the feeling of butterflies in your belly because you forgot you were supposed to brush your teeth, and you worry that I will be upset."

To encourage the development of self-regulation, watch your use of language. One word that needs careful management is "stop," as in, "Stop doing that." If you observe your own reaction to the word, you will notice "stop" momentarily gets your attention, but also may change your breathing pattern from slow and rhythmic to short and shallow. Unlike the dead-end "stop" command, true discipline teaches or suggests the appropriate behavior. For example, instead of saying, "Stop complaining," consider asking, "What do you need to feel better?" or redirect the child's attention by asking, "What is going well?"

Discipline enables your child to learn something from his actions. If your child is preoccupied with feeling unworthy or ashamed, this will overpower what he learns. To be effective, your words and body language must be delivered with respect. Respectful body language is not something you do; it is a way to feel. Some people have learned to respect others out of fear, meaning they learn to clam up and hide their emotions as a way to get through a situation. This is not the interpretation of respect being referred to here. Respecting self comes from a willingness to notice, observe, and feel your emotions. This means you will be tuning in to yourself (bodily sensations) while communicating. In order to do this well, it is important to pause between your words, soften your eyes, observe, and listen. If you are feeling heated yourself consider taking a moment to calm down before addressing your child. High levels of anger and frustration are likely to distract you away from your body (into your head). Take a moment to connect to your feet on the ground, notice your skin, and this will help center yourself so your speech can be delivered from a place of self-respect.

In order to feel respect for others, you must first learn how to respect yourself. To do this you will need to honor all of your feelings, even the ones that are uncomfortable (frustration, anger, and fear). Once you honor those emotions, you create space inside for their movement, and within that space you are able to feel the emotions that foster self-respect and compassion for others.

Family meetings are a great way to instill mindful practices that strengthen the ability to speak, listen, and observe from a state of nonreactivity. Choose to begin your meeting by taking one to three slow deep breaths. This gives everyone a chance to calm themselves down before interacting.

Once you do this you will be able to hear counterproductive language more clearly. For example, "You drive me crazy," is a signal that you may be going down a path of disrespect. Instead, keep your phrases framed in more positive "I" messages like "I feel," "I am," or "I need."

A BALANCING ACT

Your child's ability to build self-reliance is a balancing act. Encouraging independence and freedom to think endorses your values about respecting others and/or established family rules. By offering your child enough independence and freedom to explore, you can decrease dependency, fearfulness, and insecurity in your child. It will be important to constantly assess your child's changing age, developmental ability, and skills to find that balance. It is usually different for each child, and therefore important to honor individual temperaments.

Using Logical and Natural Consequences

Natural consequences are the automatic results of an action, and the parent usually plans logical consequences in advance, sometimes together with the child. Allowing logical or natural consequences to occur helps your child develop an internal understanding of self-regulation. You want your child to feel empowered and capable, which is difficult to do when you jump in and rescue your child, preventing her from experiencing her own emotions. This occurs when you make decisions for her, or resort to punishment out of fear and frustration. Choices are more hopeful and positive if you allow your child to make a decision and be responsible for the consequence for that choice. The choice then becomes a structured learning opportunity that preserves the dignity of the child, because there is no punishment or shame attached to the outcome; there is just an opportunity to take baby steps and grow in trial and error.

DOING TOO MUCH

Parents often stumble into overcompensating for their child. This can significantly affect and discourage the development of skills necessary to overcome anxiety and thrive. Although your desire is to help your child, especially when she is stressed or anxious, see it as a moment to pause. This is particularly important for tasks you know she can do for herself. Yes, sometimes it is easier to clean up for her if she is already running late, cover up her mistakes to save her self-esteem, or do her homework for her because she's having a meltdown. Children really do learn best from natural and logical consequences. Trust that this is in your child's best interest.

Logical Consequences

Logical consequences are ones that you create, based on and specifically related to an action. Three tips that help your child get the most out of logical consequences are:

- The consequence is explained ahead of time (before the behavior occurs)
- The consequence is related to the behavior
- The consequence is geared toward your child's development level

For example, if your child yells at her brother, taking her computer privileges away is a consequence that has little to do with the action that triggered it. Instead, the logical consequence would be to escort or ask your child to go to a place where she can calm down. The child may yell back or argue, and it is easy to want to respond by slipping into behavior that defends your rules and consequences. Instead, take a deep, calming breath and verbally repeat the action you wish to see the child take. In this case, you want the child to learn how to calm down, self-regulate, and to be respectful—ideally, values that you have already laid out and agreed upon. Later, when the child is calm, encourage her to apologize, or ask her to tell you what she could have said or done instead of the reaction she chose to make. Handling the situation like this teaches the child much more than lectures and quick demands do. Also, reactions such as yelling increase the likelihood that you might deliver a punishment that increases shame and blame rather than teaching a constructive lesson.

Some additional examples of logical consequences include: if your teen is disrespectful to you, she may lose the privilege of being driven to a friend's house, or if a younger child spills something, he has to clean it up (if he is under five he may need you to pitch in and help).

According to author Mark Waldman, focusing on negative words and thoughts in your speech not only releases stress hormones in your brain, but in the listener's brain as well. A simple shift in what you choose to pay attention to loosens the grip of anxiety.

One alternative that many parents and children find positive is to engage the child in the consequence. This makes your child a part of the problem-solving process, and he will feel a little less controlled. You can say to your child, "You seem to have difficulty getting yourself to bed on time; what do you think the consequence should be?" This does not mean you will do what your child says, but you can take his thoughts into account. "It feels like you are pushing for a later bedtime, which is not an option; can you think of a consequence?" Depending on your child's response, you might say, "It sounds like you feel a consequence would be to turn off the TV fifteen minutes earlier so you get yourself moving. That sounds reasonable to us."

Natural Consequences

A natural consequence is exactly what it sounds like: the natural outcome of your child's choice of behavior. Natural consequences for your child's actions are most effective when used to teach a child about responsibility. For example, when a child does not do his homework, a natural consequence will be a zero for the assignment given by the teacher, and falling behind in the class. Another example might be that if your child insists on going outside without his coat in winter, he will be cold and learn that he needs to wear the coat in order to remain warm. A natural consequence is not life threatening, and it avoids a power struggle between parent and child. These consequences allow the natural course of events to become the teacher. An example for an older child might be that if your teenager gets a speeding ticket, he will have to pay for it himself and demerit points will be assigned to his license.

Natural and logical consequences allow your child a voice, provide a tone of mutual respect, and still reinforce firm and clear guidelines.

The exceptions for using natural consequences as teaching moments are if the consequence is dangerous, the consequence will be delayed for a long time (consequences work best when immediate), or the consequence causes emotional, legal, or physical problems for other children or adults.

How Consequences Are Different from Punishment

Logical and natural consequences differ from punishment in that punishment does not teach any skills. Its intent, whether conscious or unconscious, is to make the child feel bad enough so he will never do it again. This mindset increases behaviors such as lying, avoidance, withdrawal, and anxiety. It also decreases healthy communication and the development of worthiness and capability. Punishment-related phrases sound like "You always," "You will never," "You are such a," or "Don't you ever, or else." If you were raised by punishment and find yourself going down the same path with your own children, it is strongly encouraged that you get support from a parenting class and/or therapist. Parenting classes are often available through schools, Early Childhood Family Education (ECFE) classes, libraries, and churches. Your local newspaper or school department will likely be able to assist you. If transportation or time is an issue, you can also find support online. Check the resource section at the end of this book for links and suggestions.

Parenting Dos

Following are some areas you want to strengthen, as they are known to guide children in a way that increases their autonomy and independence.

○ **Present two choices for problem solving and decision making to young children, and three to adolescents.** Teach your child that choice is one of his greatest tools. Children experiencing anxiety often have an "all or none" mode of thinking. Through discipline, you can teach them they always have more than one option. For example, you can take ten extra minutes to study, or decide against it and take the chance that you will do fine. Ultimately, natural consequences will play themselves out. Most often children learn on their own through natural consequences; however, if they repeat the behavior after receiving the consequence you may need to have a discussion with your child to help him make the connection between the action he took and the consequence he received.

○ **Deliver consequences after you calm down.** Give yourself permission to say to your child, "I am really upset right now. There will be a consequence, but first I need to calm down." Once you remove yourself from the situation, consider sitting up straight, closing your eyes, and doing some slow, deep breathing. As you inhale through your nose, drawing the breath deep into your lower belly, think of the word "let," and as you exhale, think of the word "go." Do this at least three times.

○ **Follow through on whatever consequence you choose.** Your consequence should be based on the one you are most likely to follow through with. If you say you will ground your child for three months, it is highly unlikely you will follow through with this. Avoid consequences that place a burden on you. Consider suspending one of the child's privileges. For example, if the child spends too much time on the computer, he loses the privilege of using the computer for a day or two. In some cases, computers, cell phones, and other electronic devices might have to be physically removed from the room and put out of reach to reduce conflict.

O **Intervene early.** Conflicts escalate when parents step in too late. That means the behavior goes on for quite a while before parents tend to it. Refrain from developing a habit of finishing something of your own (e.g., e-mails, texting) before attending to your child. Children notice when you are distracted, and may see it as an opportunity to get away with things. You are better off attending to the behavior in the early stages (e.g., whining) before it escalates (e.g., yelling). This increases the chance that your child will grow and learn from the experience.

O **Give your child space to grow.** When you stand over children, they will feel as if you are waiting for them to fail and do not trust them to complete the task or get through the situation alone. Persistent instructions about the right way to do things may be torturous to your child. Set realistic, obtainable goals and expectations. Most discipline is centered around teaching responsibility, but long lists of responsibilities can create pressure, anxiety, and frustration. In the beginning, focus on only two or three things. Keep them small, and gradually work on new responsibilities once the initial ones are mastered.

Positive Reinforcement

The foundation of positive reinforcement is to catch your child when she is doing something that pleases you, and then give her positive feedback about it. It is based on the premise that children's feelings of esteem and confidence are connected to, and influenced by, their relationship with their primary caregivers.

At first it may seem like a lot of work, because you need to be constantly attuned to your child's behavior in order to catch her doing something right and downplay what she is doing wrong. Research shows that, when used correctly, positive reinforcement will inspire confidence in your child and help her adopt that important "can do" attitude.

A reward happens after the fact whereas a bribe happens before. Let's say your son is afraid to go on a class trip to a waterpark. You offer to get him the new bike he wants if he faces his fears and goes. This is a bribe and not positive reinforcement. Let's say he is doing the best he can to get through his fears and chooses to go to the waterpark. He is not going to the waterpark for the reward; he is going for the pleasure of achievement. A reward is an unexpected bonus, whereas a bribe is used to motivate a child in advance. Bribes typically are not recommended, and often muddle what exactly it is that you are trying to reinforce and teach.

When you use positive reinforcement, you shift your focus from reminding your child of (and reprimanding him for) what he is doing wrong, to acknowledging his successes and showing him that he is loved, appreciated, and valued. Watch for the desired behavior to occur and then reinforce it with praise, a pat on the back for a job well done, and/or follow up with a special privilege. "Looks like your studying paid off; great job." Keep in mind that praise works best when it does not place a value on the person. There is a difference between "You are awesome" and "Great job." "You are awesome" implies the person's awesomeness is due solely to his accomplishments. Studies have shown that overly praising kids can have the reverse effect. Children and adolescents know when your comments are warranted and genuine. Adolescents in particular may feel as if you are being fake, or trying to manipulate them to act a certain way. Be genuine and matter-of-fact. A high-five, smile, thumbs-up, or verbal praise goes a long way.

ENCOURAGEMENT

Encouragement differs from praise, but is equally effective. Rather than saying "Good job," you might say, "Thank you for taking out the trash," or "I appreciate you taking the time to help your sister." Encouragement places less of a value on the person, and is a wonderful way to increase cooperation in the home environment. The bottom line is everyone likes to be noticed and appreciated for what they do, no matter how small or big it is. Parents can model appreciation through encouraging statements by supporting your parenting partner. Children learn most from what you do, as opposed to what you say.

Rewards

Rewards are based on classical conditioning. They are often used in schools and workplaces to motivate employees to go the extra mile. When using rewards, be sure the focus is on effort rather than outcome. For example, you may offer a small allowance if your child completes chores such as folding laundry and/or vacuuming. Know that it will take time for your child to master these skills, and remember that encouraging the child during the process is positive reinforcement. Also, remember that no money or item could ever replace your time and attention.

Rewards do not need to be material or cost money. Consider rewarding your child with a homemade favorite meal, trip to the park, playground, playing a game such as hide-and-seek, inviting a friend over for pizza, or a gathering around a fire pit.

The Resilient Child

Resilient children see their emotions as sources of energy, motivation, insight, and understanding. With the support of respectful discipline and encouragement, they are able to recognize the choices that support them. They learn from their mistakes instead of being crumbled by them. They possess the belief and attitude that they are worthy enough, in spite of their mishaps and stumbling blocks. A resilient child often has at least one role model in his life who illustrates the power of believing in himself. For example, this model may have a *I am strong and capable* mentality. These types of beliefs foster your child's trust in himself as well as the belief that he possesses the ability to influence the events of his life.

Resilient children recognize that their feelings, thoughts, and actions matter. They take responsibility for their mistakes, and ask for help when necessary. They break down tasks into manageable steps, focusing on the process rather than overfocusing on the outcome. They feel the rewards of their effort, rather than search for validation through external things. They choose to allow themselves to experience their emotions rather than push or shove them away. They measure their accomplishments according to their own abilities, rather than by comparing themselves to others. They see their stress and anxiety as windows of opportunity to coach their bodies and move back to the present moment.

One of the most important qualities you can instill in your children is resilience. Every child and every family is resilient. It is how well they are able to maintain their resiliency that truly makes a difference. By encouraging your child to feel and allow the experience of his emotions, you are building resiliency. Remember that emotions are not actions. As you begin to allow and feel your own emotions, this will be easier for you to teach to others. You will then be able to observe the energy of your emotions moving through your body, and breathe without judgment. Tools applied without judgment have the potential to soothe anxiety.

Important Points to Consider

You need to set limits and expectations for your child with anxiety just as you would for any of your children. However, you will need to keep some points in mind in order to discipline your child fairly:

O Your child should be made aware of what exactly is expected of her in a situation. In that way, she can know what would be appropriate behavior and what is not.

O Discipline for your child with anxiety should always aim for prevention rather than intervention. Try to address the situation before it escalates.

O Before disciplining your child, stop and try to see the situation from her point of view.

O Teach your child about logical and natural consequences. Allow her to experience the consequences of her actions so she can grow and learn.

O Focus on the issue, not the person. Your child should know that she is loved but her action is not appropriate.

O To raise your child to be independent and resilient she must experience the emotions and consequences of her actions without you stepping in or trying to protect her.

# CHAPTER 11

Self-Love

Love and anxiety cannot exist together. You cannot think or, more importantly, feel loving thoughts and be anxious. Release strategies teach your child how to free herself from lower vibrating emotions such as guilt and fear. This increases her ability to love and care for herself and by doing so she will be more equipped for supporting others.

Liberating Anxiety

Tools that bring you into the here and now can be a means of coping with anxiety as well as releasing symptoms. There are techniques and strategies that have proven to move symptoms of worry, guilt, and fear. Your child's emotions are made of energy (vibration), and the acknowledgment and movement of these emotions provides the release. As a result, your child will feel lighter, capable, and free. Consider selecting one or two releasing techniques to implement into your child's daily life. The key is not to wait until your child is anxious. Similar to brushing your teeth, release strategies work best if they are incorporated into your daily life. They can take as little as a few minutes a day. Once your child's body becomes accustomed to the practice of release, when he uses a strategy, it will be more familiar with the process and will respond according to his intention.

INTENTION

The release process always begins with an intention. Setting an intention is similar to signing a permission slip for your child to go on a field trip, only in this case, your child gives his body permission to let go of the emotions he is experiencing. To do this he will say out loud or silently, for example: *I choose to release fear, I choose to release sadness, I choose to release frustration.* After stating one or all of these, teach your child to follow the statement with a tool such as breathing or visualization. He can also set the intention nonverbally by making a physical gesture, such as closing his eyes while he breathes deeply, or placing his two feet on the ground. The body responds to both verbal and nonverbal communication.

GROUNDING

Teaching your child to ground himself before implementing a release strategy is another important factor. This can be accomplished by teaching your child to sit or stand up tall with his two feet flat on the floor. Encourage your child to lengthen his spine and hold his chin parallel to the floor. Grounding can also happen while lying flat on the floor or in bed. Because release techniques are about moving energy, you want to position your child's body in a way where this can be accomplished more easily.

Breathing

Breath work is an excellent and effective technique that you can practice anywhere and at any time. These exercises are wonderful for children of all ages once they are able to follow along, because they can be learned in a matter of a few minutes and create immediate benefits. There is also an interesting dual nature to breath work: On the one hand, breathing is automatic, and on the other hand, you can control it. For people who experience anxiety this is important, because their symptoms create a tendency to freeze up and hold their breath, increasing the feeling that things are out of control. This easy technique is a great tool and an ideal way to self-regulate.

BREATHING BASICS

Studies show a very effective way to calm yourself is to prolong your exhalation in a slow, relaxed manner. Keep that in mind when practicing the exercises that follow. Here is an example of breath work that you can do with your child. It can be done for two to ten minutes.

1. Sit in a chair with your back straight and two feet on the floor. Young children may sit on the floor cross-legged as long as they are sitting up tall with a straight spine.

2. Allow your hands to rest comfortably on your lap and let your thumb touch the middle fingertip of the same hand.

3. Close your eyes or lower your gaze toward the floor. Your chin remains parallel to the floor; just the eyes lower.

4. Begin to breathe easily and evenly, in and out, prolonging the exhalation by slowing it down. As you inhale, the lower abdomen (below the navel) should expand like a balloon or a tire tube. On exhale, the lower abdomen will contract, similar to releasing air out of tire.

5. Silently count each breath as follows: Inhale: 1, 2; exhale: 1, 2, 3. Inhale: 1, 2; exhale: 1, 2, 3. If you are doing this with your child, count out loud for her.

6. After two to three breath cycles encourage your child to sit for twenty seconds in silence and notice the sensations in her body. These are her emotions beginning to move through her body. This also teaches your child how to *receive* her breath. Receiving means taking in energy. Very often children and teens with anxiety have trained their body to give energy away through their worrisome thoughts. They deplete themselves of viable energy, which over time manifests through physical or emotional symptoms such as fear. Receiving energy on the other hand comes from tuning in to the present moment (heart and body) through observation and awareness. This replenishes your child while moving symptoms at the same time.

Teaching your child to breathe deeply in this way helps her to stimulate the vagus nerve in the lung area, which promotes physical calming. If your child gets dizzy, encourage her to exhale or take a break and resume normal breathing.

One of the gifts of moving through anxiety is the ability to learn how to receive. It is through a state of "being," rather than doing, your child will be able to foster this skill. (To learn more about receiving, read *The Four Gifts of Anxiety* by Sherianna Boyle.)

ALTERNATE NOSTRIL BREATHING

Alternate nostril breathing is an ancient technique that ties directly into your child's nervous system. The right nostril has been proven to correlate with the sympathetic nervous system, which increases alertness and arousal (similar to a cup of coffee). The left nostril corresponds with the parasympathetic nervous system, which increases relaxation (similar to a warm bath). Teach her to block off the right nostril with her thumb and breathe exclusively through the left (inhaling and exhaling) several times, slowly. By doing this she will learn how her own respiratory and nervous system are designed for both relaxation and alertness.

Follow these steps:

1. Sit up tall and close your eyes.

2. Block off the right nostril with your right thumb.

3. Inhale and exhale through the left nostril, while relaxing your jaw and shoulders. Take three or four slow inhales and exhales with the right nostril closed off. The count for inhaling and exhaling should be somewhat even in length. (If your child is sick, or suffers from allergies or respiratory conditions, avoid this technique until she is better.)

SIGNS THAT BREATH WORK IS WORKING

When practicing breath work, it is typical for both adults and children to experience some bodily discomfort. Know that these are signs that what you are doing is working. Some of these physical signs include shifting in the seat, looking around the room, restlessness, and difficulty concentrating. When the brain is introduced to something new, it initially moves through some discomfort, evidenced through the body. Stay calm, be patient, and trust that the breath and body know what to do. These experiences may be similar to the edginess your child feels when she is anxious. As your child experiences discomfort in meditation or breath work, she becomes familiar with how to use it to move emotion in daily life.

PLAYFUL BREATHING

There are many fun ways to present breathing techniques to children. A simple way is to get a bottle of bubbles from a toy store, or have your child pretend to blow bubbles. The breathing required is the same as for the calm breathing technique, but you can have fun trying to see who can blow the biggest bubble. This takes long, slow, steady breaths, which increases relaxation. You can then tell her that any time she feels anxious, she can say to herself, "I do not need to worry, I can pretend to blow bubbles and feel better!"

Other creative ways for teaching young children how to breathe in a controlled, relaxed manner are to imagine they are blowing on hot food or blowing out a candle.

Books that teach young children about relaxation can be wonderful guides (for example, *Relax* by Catherine O'Neill). Adolescents and children may enjoy listening to a relaxing CD or app. The website *www.stressfreekids.com* provides CDs and books for children, teens, and adults.

Meditation

Meditation is a way to train the mind to calm down, focus, and pay attention. It allows you to access your higher consciousness, which is the part of you that is able to trust and make choices that are in your best interest as well as your child's. When your mind is busy with mental chatter, your body is not able to optimally utilize its resources that promote healing, attention, and connection. Busy thoughts keep your brain on alert and focused on the future. Meditation also creates an alert brain, yet accomplishes this by focusing on the here and now. The difference is in how your body responds. When you are future-focused, your body can become tense, tight, and distracted. Present focus, on the other hand, allows you to relax, feel, and sense what is happening without taxing the body, keeping it in emergency (anxiety) mode when there is no pending threat.

BEGINNING MEDITATION

In the beginning, your meditation practice may be a few minutes long. Duration of practice is not as important as frequency. Therefore, it is better to practice a few minutes daily, rather than for thirty minutes once a week. Many people associate meditation with religion or sitting on the floor. Meditation can take on a variety of forms and can be applied while moving or sitting still. You can learn how to meditate while walking, drinking tea, biking, or even while you do the dishes. Any time you are observing your breath and body through conscious and loving awareness, meaning your intention is to support yourself in a kind way, you are meditating.

Your intention is not to get rid of or stop your thoughts. Your thoughts are part of being human; they will continue, however, as you breathe and focus on the sensations in your body, which are delivered through your sense of smell, touch, hearing, sight, and perception of temperature and balance. In time, you will find the frequency of your thoughts decrease. You will also find that the quality of your thoughts will change from fearful to compassion-based.

Meditation decreases stress, pulse rate, blood pressure, metabolism, and muscle tension while enhancing mood and helping you feel more peaceful. You become more in touch with your body, which helps you to get an honest and accurate read of your stress and anxiety levels. It also increases memory, improves circulation, the ability to pay attention, and supports the overall immune system.

It is recommended that you practice meditating yourself before attempting to teach it to your child. To begin, start by applying it to something you already do, for example, doing the dishes or folding the laundry. As you begin the task, notice your eyes. Begin to soften your gaze (as if you had sleepy eyes). You may have to close them for a few seconds and reopen them. Next, relax the corners of your mouth and separate your back teeth. Notice if your lips are pursed, and if so separate them slightly. Relax your jaw and forehead. This may take up to thirty seconds. Then place your two feet on the floor either while sitting or standing. Begin to notice yourself balancing between your two feet. Press them into the floor until you feel securely grounded.

As you take these small actions you are already in the process of meditating. When you go about your day with mental awareness, meditation is activated. Now, while folding the laundry, you might notice the texture and smell of the clothes and how they feel on the palm of your hand. You may gaze out the window and watch the birds or hear the wind, or you may choose to simply focus on breathing in and out without judgment. Just by noticing that you are breathing, you are meditating.

TEACHING MEDITATION TO YOUR CHILD

Once you practice on yourself and become a role model, you can begin to guide your child. Note that there is no one way to do this. In the beginning, you may need to sit with your child alone and simply breathe together. Some children do well lying in bed while listening to relaxing sounds. Getting outside in nature and taking a walk without trying to occupy the space with conversation also works. Just allowing your child to feel, breathe, and be free is one of the natural ways to invite meditation into your life.

Before beginning meditation, encourage your child to set an intention. For example, *I choose to release stress, I choose to focus on the here and now, I choose to release nervousness.* If your child is young you can set the intention for him and model by sitting next to him. Encourage him to relax his shoulders, jaw, hips, and thighs. As this occurs, your child's breath will naturally expand. Now he is positioned for a release and practicing meditation.

Progressive Muscle Relaxation

Progressive muscle relaxation, or PMR, is a two-step process of deliberately applying tension to certain muscle groups, contracting them, and then releasing the muscle and observing it as it relaxes. The object of this technique is to help you and your child quickly learn to recognize what a tensed muscle and a completely relaxed muscle feel like. You can do this with any body part, such as the hands, feet, and facial muscles. PMR works well when your body is craving physical stimulation. For example, children who feel like they are crawling out of their own skin, wiggly, or distracted often do well with PMR and breath work together.

HOW TO PERFORM PMR

It is best to practice PMR in a quiet, comfortable place, wearing loose-fitting clothing and no shoes. Your child can lie down, but as is common with these types of exercises, it increases the chance that you or your child may fall asleep. Therefore, unless that is the goal, it may be better to sit in a comfortable chair. This is the process:

1. Starting with his toes, your child should tighten the muscles in his toes and hold for a count of five. Then let go, and observe and enjoy the release for thirty seconds.

2. Next, he should tighten the muscles in his feet and hold for a count of five. Again, he should relax through the release for a count of thirty.

3. Continue by moving slowly up through his body: contracting and releasing each leg, his abdomen, back, neck, face, and eyes.

4. With each body part, he should breathe through the muscle work deeply and slowly.

5. You can even have your child lift his arms over his head and squeeze his fists tight, and then release and lower them by his side. Have your child imagine the tension is in the palm of his hand, squeeze it tight, and then exhale and let it go.

6. After he has finished with his entire body, he should relax with his eyes closed for a few seconds, then get up slowly and stretch.

Creative Visualizations

Physician and author Martin L. Rossman says there is enough evidence to make the case that "the human imagination is the most powerful force on earth." Your child's imagination is one of her greatest tools. By visualizing calming or empowering scenes, she has the ability to change her current state of mind from the experience of fear, dread, or feeling overwhelmed to feeling tranquil, lucid, and peaceful.

HOW IMAGERY WORKS

Your mind and body are connected, and if you use all your senses, your body can respond as if what you imagine is real. Creative imagery brings the visualization to life. By encouraging your child to engage all her senses, your child's body believes it is truly happening. For example, if your child imagines she is releasing stress by visualizing a vacuum sucking the stress of her day out of her head while breathing and relaxing her jaw, this in turn creates a physiological response in the body. Her blood may flow more freely as her sensations increase circulation. Release strategies can be fun and give your child the freedom to be creatively empowered.

A VISUALIZATION EXAMPLE

Practical visualizations such as releasing a jam from a photocopy machine provide your child or teen with a more concrete way of understanding how release strategies work. Picture making a copy of a piece of paper. The machine needs to scan the entire piece of paper in order to make the copy. If the paper becomes jammed, it won't work. This is similar to an emotion. To fully release an emotion from the body, it is important to experience it from beginning to middle to end. This works even if the emotion is from the past. Encourage your child to visualize her breath by tuning in to be consciously aware of the beginning, middle, and end of the breath. She could also mentally scan her body from beginning to middle to end; she may begin at the top of her head and then drop her awareness to her face, neck, shoulders, chest, arms, midsection, legs, knees, feet, and floor as she exhales slowly. On the inhale, she will travel her awareness back up to the top of her head. This can be done in twenty seconds and teaches your child how to move her own energy (remember, emotions are energy).

Guided Imagery

Guided imagery uses a more formal method to direct your thoughts and guide your imagination toward relaxation. Guided visualizations can be found on iTunes or may be purchased as an app to be played on your smartphone, on DVD, or on CD. Clinically based relaxation and guided visualization MP3s and apps may also be found at online shops such as *www.heartmath.com*. Imagery works well for children because they do not have to think; they can just sit back, close their eyes, and let a soothing voice take them to a calm, relaxing place through a gentle story. Guided imagery has also been useful with children who have difficulty falling asleep, or staying asleep, because of anxiety. It allows children and teens to turn off their minds and fall into a deep and peaceful sleep while listening to beautiful music, the sounds of nature, and a calming, affirming story.

Self-Talk

In education as well as in parenting, a great deal of attention is given to how to talk to other people. This section focuses on teaching children how to talk to themselves in a way that diminishes anxiety. People generally don't share the thoughts that are going on in their head, particularly if they are stressful in nature. When your child tells you about a fear, stressful situation, or event, consider asking, "What were your thoughts telling you in that moment?" Some children may not let you know what is going on inside of their head because they do not wish to disappoint or burden you. Also, if they are always hearing how stressed or anxious you are, they may be more in tune with your words rather than their own.

TRUTH STATEMENTS

Truth statements are a way to redirect your child's thinking from counterproductive worrying to more productive states of being. They acknowledge what is happening in the moment while creating a hopeful future. Truth statements keep expectations simple and realistic. Some examples of truth statements are:

- I notice I am expecting to feel some worry over this, but I choose to free myself from these expectations.

- This may seem hard now, but it will become easier and easier over time.

- When this is over, I will be glad that I did it.

- I have more influence over these thoughts and feelings than I once imagined.

- These feelings are uncomfortable. They will be over with soon, and I will be fine.

- Learning how to live with stress shows how capable I am.

Repeated regularly (daily or weekly) over time will begin to reprogram the computer (brain) in your child's head to fit the life she wants, and create the momentum needed to be the person she is.

From Worrywart to Worry Warrior

Children or adults with anxiety are sometimes called "worrywarts." Names like this prevent children from seeing themselves in another more positive way. These types of labels are often a reflection of parental anxiety, or in some cases used by siblings who think that feelings are something you make fun of or push away. The term worrywart is typically applied to someone who overreacts to small mistakes, is doubtful, and dreads outcomes he cannot control.

WORRY WARRIORS

Worry warriors are able to see their thoughts as something that can be managed and released by their breath and body. To help your child see himself as a worry warrior, refrain from messages that indicate you are trying to get rid of the worry. You don't get rid of worries; you *recycle* them. This means that through body awareness and breathing, worries get converted into beneficial emotions that serve your child well. You cannot recycle what you don't want or have. Each time your child pauses to observe his body and breathing, he is sending that worry through a process of change.

PRESS DELETE

Just as you can reframe or change the cover photo on your phone, kids can be taught how to do this with their thoughts as well. Younger children may relate to this technique more through drawing. For example, you can write or draw your worry and then practice erasing it. Have your child exhale while erasing it so he can actually feel the thought leaving his body. Worry warriors understand that they can change their "cover photo," meaning that when they hear a voice in their head that says something negative or fearful, they have the power to change it. All they have to do is take a breath and speak to that fearful part of self, saying something like "change," "cancel," or "delete." Encourage them to use a warrior tone of voice when they speak to themselves. Say it like a command, and the thought will be canceled. When they do this, they are making space for their positive voice to surface and be heard.

HELPING YOUNG CHILDREN TO BE WORRY WARRIORS

Young children may find it hard to understand what you mean by "recycle your worries," and therefore will not be able to comprehend how to apply the strategy. A fun approach to try would be to play a question game. As you read a book with pictures together, stop and ask at each picture, "Hmm, I wonder what she is thinking? What would be your guess?" If your child struggles at the beginning, help him work it through by examining different aspects of the picture. "Well, let's see if we can tell by her eyes, or her face," you might say. "What do you think her arms are telling us, crossed like that?" This allows you the opportunity to help your child identify possibilities, positive ones as well as negative, in an effort to understand his own feelings better. Then talk about how to say a keyword like "Stop" or "Erase" and replace the negative thought, with something like this: "Yes, her eyes do look worried. Do you think she is worried that her dad will miss her game? Maybe she can say 'Stop' to herself and remember that he has never missed a game yet, and he helps her practice all the time, so he either is on his way or has a very good reason if he does not show up. What else do you think she could say to herself to make herself feel better?" This approach is also a great way to help children identify feelings and identify the difference between a thought and a feeling, which can be difficult for younger children.

Self-Soothing Strategies

It is essential that you and your child learn how to care for yourselves with techniques that can calm anxiety. Meditation, breathing exercises, prayer, physical exercise, a warm bath, unstructured play, getting involved in a hobby you enjoy, and getting together with friends all soothe the busyness of the mind. Preteens and adolescents often report music being one of their most popular forms of stress relief. Be sure your child's music includes positive, nonviolent lyrics and messages. Connecting to nature is also a natural way to reset the rhythm of the body. Interacting with animals is a great source for stress relief, as well as creativity and laughter. When weather keeps you indoors, consider playful activities such as a balloon toss, dancing, fine motor activities such as building with Lego, and arts and crafts. Here are some additional well-researched and documented self-soothing strategies.

CHANTING

Chanting is an ancient technique that uses specific sounds made with your own voice, or listening to the chanting of others, to alter the neurochemistry of the brain. Since your body is made up of 80–90 percent water, certain repeated sounds can impact your body on a cellular level. According to the article "The Healing Power of Sound and Overtone Chant" by Nestor Kornblum, chants (such as *sat nam*) create "higher rate of vibration [which] creates large spaces between cells, making us less dense, and preventing negative or intrusive energies from sticking to us easily." (*Sat* in Sanskrit means truth and *nam* means name; "truth is in my name.") You can also have children practice and feel the benefits of sound by chanting vowel sounds.

Chants are available for downloading online or for purchase on iTunes, and playing chant music can be an effective way to break up any negative energy in your home.

CHIMES, BELLS, CRYSTAL BOWLS

Tibetan singing bowls, gongs, wooden chimes, and crystal bowls reverberate when struck, creating a long-lasting sound wave that can release tension in the body. You can also purchase these sounds in an app and adjust them to ring randomly on your phone or at certain scheduled times of day to remind you to take a deep breath and refocus your awareness on your body. Children and adolescents are often curious about sounds, and may be more interested than you expect.

TAPPING

Tapping (also referred to as EFT, Emotional Freedom Technique) is a healing technique partially based on acupressure, and done using the tips of your fingers. Specific points in the body are tapped with the fingers to increase and promote the circulation of energy. One of those points is called the karate chop and is located between the base of the pinky and the wrist. Using two fingers on the other hand, your child can tap the point repeatedly for one to two minutes while stating, "Even though I feel nervous or worried, I completely and totally love and accept myself." More information regarding tapping points can be found online, and also in Nick Ortner's book, *The Tapping Solution*.

MUDRAS

Mudras are a position of your body (often the hands and fingers) that have been found to direct energy in a specific direction. Different mudras have been found to correspond to different energy centers in the body, often referred to as chakras. Chakras are areas in the body where energy pools together. For example, if you want to stimulate peace, there is a specific hand position (incorporated with breathing and awareness) that will help stimulate the flow in certain areas of the body such as the abdomen, heart, and throat. When this energy is flowing in these areas, physical and emotional well-being are found to be impacted in a positive way.

Marsha Therese Danzig's book *Children's Book of Mudras* is a resource for parents looking to use this technique with their children to help manage anxiety.

The tips of your fingers have more nerve endings than any other part of your body. They can connect to different parts your body while engaging in deep breathing. According to Amy Weintraub, author of *Yoga Skills for Therapists*, "After centuries of study, it is understood that each finger, the pressure applied, and the direction it faces, correspond to different areas of the body, the brain, and the emotions. Certain mudras lift mood, while others calm it." One mudra that promotes calm is pressing the pad of the uppermost joint of your two middle fingers, two inches above your navel, with your palms facing up. You can even add the sound of *ahhhhhh* while pressing them. Hold the mudra for a few rounds of breathing.

MANTRAS

Mantras are words or phrases used when your mind is quiet or during meditation. *Man* means mind, while *tra* refers to what frees the mind. They can help you and your child shift from a state of fear into love. Studies show when repeated for several minutes, mantras balance the right and left brain. Parents can also state mantras for their child. Some examples of mantras are: *Peace radiates through me, I am love, Let go*, or *So hum* (I am that). You can also create specific mantras to help your child through situations. Some examples are: *Good grades come easily, Taking tests comes with ease, Making friends comes naturally*, and/or *Studying strengthens me*. Mantras work best when repeated nine or ten times in a row in the morning and at night.

REIKI

Reiki is another technique that you can do on yourself or your child. You can use the palm of your hand to move congested energy in the body, creating a sense of peace and inner balance. Parents can do Reiki on their children before they go to bed to help promote a good night's sleep. While breathing deeply, move your hand in a clockwise circular motion a few inches above your child's heart or belly. This is best done in a dimly lit room, away from distractions. Reiki classes are offered frequently in communities by yoga studios, massage therapists, and nurses.

ENERGY MEDICINE

Energy medicine has been around for thousands of years. Psychologist David Feinstein and energy healer Donna Eden have been among the pioneers who have brought this incredible tool to modern life. Like acupressure, it involves tapping and tracing pathways (meridians) of energy. One of the ideas behind this technique is to get the blood flowing between hemispheres of the brain. This can be achieved by exercises such as having your child march in place while slapping the hand to her opposite knee. You can also have your child rub her hands together to create friction. The heat created is a form of energy. Next, have her bring the palm of one hand (either one) and hovering it about two inches above her forehead, take one to two slow deep (lower belly) breaths. This stimulates blood flow in the forehead (which is where your forebrain is located) while sending calming signals to the nerves. Parents interested in learning simple practices might consider reading *The Little Book of Energy Medicine* by Donna Eden.

BIRTHDAY CANDLE EXERCISE

This technique can be taught to children of all ages. Have your child hover her hand two inches from her forehead (palm facing the head) and inhale. As she exhales, she will move her hand down to in front of her throat area and inhale. On exhale, she will lower it to her heart and inhale. Have her repeat the breath cycle as she slowly moves her hand down to two inches above her navel, and then to two inches below her navel. Now, add the visualization of lighting birthday candles. Do this exercise twice, the first without the visualization of the candles and the second with. The first candle is the forehead and her hand, representing the candle's flame, will light the remaining energy centers. These energy centers, or chakras, are where energy pools in the body. It is not necessary to coordinate the breath with the physical action and the visualization. As long as she is inhaling and exhaling in somewhat equal lengths and her hand travels as she exhales, this technique will work.

WARMTH AND SMELL

Similar to when you soothed your child as an infant by swaddling her or wrapping her in your arms and drawing her close, wrapping yourself or your child in a warm blanket fresh out of the dryer can help soothe the nervous system. Making sure your child is exposed to natural sunlight for at least ten minutes daily is also essential, as light supports the production of vitamin D in the body. Vitamin D helps regulate the absorption of calcium in your bones and supports cell-to-cell communication, which is essential to the nervous system. Yummy homemade soup can also ease and warm the nerves in your child's tummy.

Smell is one of the quickest ways to soothe your mood. It is equally important to monitor harsh or toxic smells that may bother your child. Some household products can cause headaches and irritability, some examples being harsh cleaning products, laundry detergent, deodorant, and perfumes.

Important Points to Consider

For your child living with anxiety, finding ways to relax and soothe his body is critical to getting a hold on anxious feelings. You can help your child by teaching him ways to pause and release the hold anxiety has on him. When looking into release strategies, keep these important points in mind:

O Different strategies will work in varying degrees for your child. Because each child is an individual with unique anxiety issues, your child may have to try several techniques before he finds the one that is best for him.

O Teach your child to give his body permission to let go of the anxious or negative emotions he is experiencing.

O When your child is anxious he may freeze or hold his breath, which in turn increases his anxiety. By teaching your child deep-breathing techniques, you help him self-regulate his body.

O Help your child focus on the here and now when he is anxious. Meditation can give your child the present focus he needs to feel, relax, and understand that there is no pending threat.

O Teaching your child truth statements will help redirect his thinking from worrying to more productive states of being.

O Sometimes just imagining the anxiety being taken out of his body can bring a relaxing effect to your child. Teach him how to use creative imagery to influence the pull that anxiety has on his mind.

 **CHAPTER 12**

Self-Love Living: Exercise, Nutrition, and Sleep

Proper nutrition, sleep, and adequate physical exercise are a large part of your child's self-love living. Anxiety is what happens when stress is left unattended, creating a disconnect between the mind, body, and spirit. Unhealthy habits such as overusing technology and mindless eating contribute to making it difficult for your child to pick up on her internal cues. Creating healthy habits to replace them steers your child back on track with a deeper understanding of her own bodily needs.

Simple Ways to Curb Anxiety

There are several easy antidotes for minor or temporary anxiety, which are effective for children at almost any age. These remedies, many based on traditional systems of healing, are noninvasive, largely inexpensive, and easy to implement.

MAINTAIN BLOOD SUGAR

According to nutritionist Jack Challem, author of *The Food-Mood Solution*, maintaining stable blood sugar levels through regular meals or small snacks that are rich in protein and mood-enhancing nutrients (omega-3 fats) helps decrease levels of anxiety. To do this, consider making foods for breakfast that you might typically eat for lunch, such as a slice of low-salt turkey, vegetable soup, tofu smoothies, or whole-grain or gluten-free bread with coconut butter or almond butter. Include an extra snack for when your child rides home on the bus or in the car.

EXAMINE THE DAIRY/WHEAT DILEMMA

Some children are sensitive to the way dairy is pasteurized. If your child sounds congested or struggles with allergies, this compiled with stress can contribute to overall anxiety levels. Consider substituting with nondairy alternatives such as almond milk, coconut milk, or soy. These are also rich in vitamin B, which is a mood-enhancing supplement.

Consider having your child tested for gluten or wheat intolerance. According to Dr. Stephen Wangen, "It has been well established that a gluten intolerance can dramatically affect the skin, nervous system, musculoskeletal system, immune system, energy level, joints, teeth, and even behavior and mood."

TEA TIME

Tea has long been used worldwide as an herbal and social remedy for calming the mind, improving digestive problems, and other positive effects on the body. Chamomile is one of the most popular teas for encouraging sleep; passionflower, lemon balm, and jasmine are also purported to have soothing effects. The warming sensation of the tea, enjoyed in a quiet environment, is a healthy way for your child to wind down at the end of the day. It is also a nice accompaniment to reading or doing homework. Even the ritual of preparing the tea can be grounding, if it is done mindfully. Just remember to check to be sure that it does not contain caffeine!

BATH

Bathing has been used for millennia in many cultures to promote health, hygiene, spiritual purification, and even socialization. The calming effect of the warm water, especially when combined with aromatic soaps and oils, music, and soft lighting, can alleviate anxiety and help with insomnia. Many parents use bathing as a part of the bedtime ritual. For younger children especially, bath time can be excellent for bonding, a time to incorporate massage, or even breathing and visualization. Use your intuition, though, to make sure combining more than one approach at a time is not overly stimulating. You can encourage older children to use bathing independently for calming purposes, and also to reduce insomnia.

SHAKE AND DANCE

This technique uses the body's activity to help the mind let go of tension, anxiety, and worry. All it requires is music, a few minutes, and the ability to let go of self-consciousness. To start, find some lively music with a good beat that you think your child would enjoy, or, depending on age, ask your child to pick a piece of music to "get the jitters out."

Play the music, and begin to very deliberately shake your body (do this with your child). Shake your hands, feet, arms, legs, head, torso, eyes, tongue, hair, and anything else you can! Do this for at least a minute or two; it's okay if you can't do the whole song. If you like, after shaking, you can then switch the music to something soaring, happy, uplifting, or calming.

You and your child will both be surprised at how different you feel after this exercise, and the laughter that can result is good medicine in itself! Make it a regular part of your routine and older children are less likely to resist it.

Foods That Can Increase Anxiety

Just as a healthy diet can relieve symptoms of anxiety, some foods can worsen mood symptoms because of their effects on the body's biochemistry. If your child feels anxious, you may wish to restrict or eliminate sugar, caffeine, some starches, wheat, and processed foods.

CAFFEINE

Most people know that caffeine is a stimulant that can cause jitteriness, irritability, and anxiety, but many do not know about hidden sources of caffeine. Many sodas and sports drinks contain caffeine. Energy drinks, even if advertised as natural, may also contain caffeine. Caffeine is also present in cocoa, chocolate, and some teas. If your child has trouble sleeping, be sure to limit sources of caffeine at least four hours before bedtime. You may wish to eliminate caffeine entirely from your child's diet when anxiety is a concern.

SUGAR

Many parents are familiar with the hyperactivity, and possible energy and emotional crash, which results from your child's excessive sugar consumption at Halloween, Valentine's Day, parties, or other occasions when sweets are center stage. Sugar in and of itself has no nutritional value other than simple calories. When ingested, it can cause a quick surge in energy, which can then be followed by a "crash" marked by tiredness, lethargy, or even emotionality and irritability.

Look at food labels closely. Many yogurts have the same amount of sugar as a can of soda. Greek yogurt typically has half the sugar, compared to regular yogurt. Also, you can purchase plain yogurt and teach your child how to sweeten her own food with natural honey and organic sugar. Teach your child how to read nutritional information labels closely, paying attention to serving sizes.

For some children, the energy surge caused by sugary foods or drinks can mimic a panic attack. You may wish to limit your child's sugar intake to help with anxiety. To sweeten foods more naturally, with a gentler effect on mood and energy, consider fruit juice, stevia (an herbal sweetener available at most health food stores), or honey, if your child is over two years old. Remember that fresh fruit is a natural, healthy, and satisfying option for dessert. Be alert to "disguised sugar" in the form of high-fructose corn syrup and sucrose, which are common in many processed foods. Also, be aware of added sugar in foods like breads, crackers, and spaghetti or other sauces.

CARBOHYDRATES

Carbohydrates are essential for the production of energy, and all people need some carbs to be healthy. In fact, taking carbohydrates out of your diet completely can interfere with your intestinal tract. Carbohydrate intake can be increased when physical demands increase; take, for example, the athlete who eats a huge spaghetti dinner or pancake breakfast before a competition. However, if your child's diet is too high in carbohydrates, he may experience extreme fluctuations in mood and energy, and may be prone to periods of anxiety. This is because carbohydrates quickly metabolize into the sugars (glucose) the body uses for energy. When the sugar burns off, a crash in energy, with accompanying malaise, distress, irritability, "spaciness," or moodiness, can occur.

Conditions like hypoglycemia or diabetes are dependent on good management of carbohydrate intake. Starch alternatives such as brown rice pasta, quinoa, or gluten-free products may be easier to digest, easing the highs and lows.

PROTEIN

Increasing the amount of high-protein foods in the diet has been found to stabilize and elevate mood, and increase energy. Remember to use lean sources of protein such as fish, turkey, and chicken, and avoid meats high in fat, sodium, nitrates, or other additives. Adding protein to a meal or snack heavy in carbohydrates slows the metabolization of glucose and prevents a "crash." If your child has trouble staying asleep, this may be due to a carb crash signaling her body that she needs more calories. Try offering a small serving of protein (nuts or nut butters, meat, cheese, yogurt) before bed to see if this helps.

Vitamins and Nutritional Supplements

There is much controversy about the safety and efficacy of vitamins, herbs, enzymes, and nutritional supplements. The 1994 Dietary Supplement Health and Education Act (DSHEA) restricts the FDA's authority over supplements, provided that companies do not claim their products treat, prevent, or cure disease. As such, the FDA views nutritional supplements as foods that contain ingredients intended to supplement the diet.

Many professionals, including the American Academy of Pediatrics, warn against giving supplements to children to make up for an uneven diet. It's always better for children to meet their nutritional needs through food. However, individuals low in vitamins and minerals such calcium, magnesium, and vitamin B can show signs of anxiety. You can find accurate and useful information on supplements at the National Institutes of Health (*www.nih.gov*) and the National Center for Complementary and Integrative Health (*www.nccih.nih.gov*).

Check with your child's doctor or a qualified naturopathic or homeopathic physician before starting a supplementation program. The doctor will help you determine proper dosing for your child's age, and check on potential medication interactions, side effects, or other precautions.

HERBS

Herbal or botanical supplements are dietary supplements that are used for a medicinal purpose. They generally support a specific aspect of the body's health, such as the heart, bones, or digestive system. However, just because a product is labeled as "natural" does not mean that it is safe or without side effects. In fact, many herbal supplements can produce strong effects in the body, particularly if taken improperly or at high doses.

People with anxiety should be especially careful when using herbal formulas. Remember also that the levels of standardization in dosing, labeling, and added ingredients are not regulated by the FDA in the same way that pharmaceutical products are, and can be dangerous to infants and children.

Herbs that have been safely used with children include: St. John's Wort, hops, L-theanine, holy basil, passionflower, skullcap, valerian, and oat straw. Research also shows that kava, L-theanine, and holy basil can reduce anxiety. However, you should do some research before administering herbs, to check dosages, interactions, and possible side effects. Again, consulting with a medical professional can be a good idea before beginning an herbal course of treatment.

VITAMINS

Vitamin supplements provide extra supplies of micronutrients the body needs for growth, digestion, and mood regulation. Different food sources contain different vitamins and minerals, and a wide and varied diet is the best way to make sure you and your child get enough of them. Supplements can be used in special conditions, under the care and advice of a qualified physician. Vitamins and minerals that are especially important in managing mood and anxiety include:

O **B vitamins:** Effective in helping maintain adequate serotonin levels, which improve mood and combat the effects of stress. These vitamins lessen the body's tendency to become overstimulated by adrenaline, such as might occur in panic attacks or prolonged states of anxiety associated with PTSD. A good B-complex supplement should contain the essential B vitamins, which are thiamin, riboflavin, niacin, vitamin B_6, vitamin B_{12}, and pantothenic acid. Generally, B vitamins are found in meat, fish, garlic, sunflower seeds, grains, legumes, liver, bananas, and some dairy products.

- **Vitamin D:** Supports normal levels of calcium and phosphorus; found in cod liver oil, fish (salmon), fortified dairy products, eggs, and sun exposure.

- **Vitamin C:** Antioxidant that supports the health and growth of connective tissue, nervous tissue, and mitochondria, and is plentiful in citrus fruits and green veggies (e.g., Brussels sprouts). Over-the-counter products like powders and chewable tablets are convenient and kid-friendly.

MINERAL SUPPLEMENTS

Mineral supplements provide micronutrients found extensively in bone and teeth. In addition, minerals help the body create new cells and enzymes, distribute fluids, control nerve impulses, and bring oxygen to cells while taking away carbon dioxide. One important mineral to help regulate anxiety is magnesium. Magnesium can relax nerves and muscles, and is a natural sleep-inducing element found in legumes, dark leafy vegetables, almonds, and whole grains.

According to Mark Mincolla, PhD, author of *Whole Health*, emotional overeating or undereating can lead to serious anxiety conditions such as eating disorders. He suggests thinking of eating disorders as a heartache disorder and encourages supports that teach your child how to feel the pain, rather than "feeding it down."

ESSENTIAL FATTY ACIDS

Essential fatty acids (EFAs), sometimes referred to as omega-3s, are natural nutrients that improve communication between brain cells. Their importance in cardiovascular health has been clearly established, and there is good research supporting the use of EFAs/omega-3s to manage anxiety, depression, and bipolar disorder. EFAs are available in cold-water fish such as salmon, tuna, trout, and others, as well as in avocado. Flaxseed oil contains alpha-linolenic acid, which converts to the EFAs found in fish oils. There are many health benefits to increasing fish in the diet, and flax-seed oil is easy to incorporate into the diet as well. The size of the capsules can be daunting for children, so you may have to add the oil to a food. Some products (especially flax) need refrigeration, and many people can't take fish oils without other food, due to stomach upset and "fish breath." If either occurs on a regular basis, consider changing your child's supplement or switching to flax.

Exercise and Yoga

Exercise, including yoga, alleviates mental stress, increases blood flow to the brain, improves mood, energy, and sleep, and can create an overall sense of well-being. It can provide distraction from emotional distress, help your child tune in to her body, and enhance her sense of physical strength, endurance, mastery, and confidence.

EXERCISE GUIDELINES

The 2008 USDA and Department of Health and Human Services guidelines recommend that all children six years and older should get sixty minutes of moderate to vigorous exercise on most, if not all, days of the week. Exercise should include the components of endurance, strength, and flexibility, and should involve both structured and free play. Encourage regular exercise to help your anxious child optimize mood-boosting brain chemistry, and to "blow off steam." However, if your child has trouble sleeping, she should avoid exercise within two to four hours before bedtime because it can be overly stimulating.

YOGA

Yoga is an ancient meditation practice with Eastern roots that involves quieting the mind and using various body postures to attain a greater sense of balance and control and create a sense of well-being. One of the best postures you can teach your child is the standing mountain pose. This pose teaches your child how to become centered and grounded into her body, which is important as children experiencing anxiety are often caught up in their thoughts.

To do standing mountain pose, stand up tall with your feet parallel on the floor and your arms by your side. If you are leaning forward into your knees, gently shift yourself between the balls of your feet and heels, roll your shoulders back and down, and keep your chin parallel to the floor. Engage your legs by lifting up your kneecaps through your quadriceps muscles as well as a lift in the inner thighs by pressing the heels of both feet gently on the floor. Soften your eyes by dropping your gaze (not your chin) to the floor and open your palms so you can receive your breath.

Child's pose is another pose your child can try. Have your child get down on the floor on all fours and then move her hips back until they land on her heels and place her forehead on the floor or a pillow. Run your hand down her spine. As you do this imagine fluid moving freely up and down the spine, clearing the mental toxins from the day.

Many communities have yoga centers that offer classes for children and/or families. Check your local bookstore or library for children's yoga tapes, CDs, and DVDs.

A third posture is to have your child lie down on her back and place her legs up a wall. Have her be far enough from the wall to lie comfortably. With her arms down by her sides, ask her to close her eyes and feel her breath rising and falling. Tell her to blow up her belly like a balloon as she inhales and deflate toward the spine as she exhales. Have her do this anywhere from three to ten minutes in a space that is relatively quiet. She could even listen to relaxing music on her iPod while doing this.

These three basic yoga poses can help to alleviate anxiety. One or all three poses along with slow conscious breathing (two or three long inhales, followed by three long exhales) can make a huge difference when practiced daily.

Sleep Routine and Ritual

It is very common for children with anxiety to have trouble transitioning into sleep, sleeping independently, and falling and staying asleep. One of the purposes of sleep is to help your child recover from the stressors of the day.

Children who are sensitive to anxiety are known to easily absorb the tension and the emotions of others from their surroundings. It will be important for your child to recognize and accept this about himself and create rituals that support him in letting go before attempting to go to sleep.

On average, doctors recommend children from birth to age six need ten to thirteen hours of sleep, ages six to nine need ten hours, ages ten through twelve need nine hours, and adolescents need eight to nine hours.

LETTING GO OF THE DAY

At the end of the day before bed, or even when he gets home from school, encourage your child to create his own ritual for letting go of anxiety. Often children and adolescents associate the end of the day with tasks like homework or chores, or with activities like sports practice. Most parents would agree the days are filled with physical, emotional, and mental demands. Having your child create a letting-go ritual is a way to teach him how to let go of the day's demands and lingering thoughts and feelings.

The most important part of a letting-go ritual is the intention. An intention is a way to determine how you will act or what will take place in the moment. It is different from a goal because it focuses on the present moment. For example, while performing the ritual of washing his hands your child might imagine that negativity, stress, and pressure are being washed away. He could also state a mantra to himself while washing his hands. For example, *I choose to keep all the positive energy and let go of all the negative energy.* Or he could say, *Letting go of what I don't need and appreciating what I do comes easily.*

Allow your child to be creative and incorporate it into something he might already do. For example, your child could walk the dog, jump on a trampoline, or practice shooting a basketball. Each time he gets the basketball in the hoop he could imagine dunking the stressors of the day.

Some children might benefit from keeping a journal of what they are choosing to release, as well as what they would like to increase in their life. For example, *I am choosing to release anger and increase love.* Keep in mind it is the intention of letting go that makes this a powerful ritual, rather than getting the words right.

When you talk to or about your child, try not to say things like "your anxiety" or "my child's anxiety." It's better to talk about individual symptoms like nervousness, self-doubt, or insecurity. For example, you might say something like "Hannah felt nervous before the test," or "It sounds like you felt nervous before the test." Breaking down the symptoms makes releasing them at the end of the day less overwhelming.

WINDING DOWN

Help your child find ways to ramp down his level of physical, mental, and emotional stimulation so that he can drop off to sleep easily and naturally. One hour or more before bedtime, you can help your child to wind down by having him finish homework and computer gaming time, lowering the volume on music, shutting down screen time, and dimming the lights. Avoiding TV, computers, or video games maximizes the production of sleep hormones. Reading, telling stories, and listening to music can be good transition activities, but make sure that your child avoids watching or listening to anything aggressive. A gentle side stretch (arms overhead, stretching side to side) before bed can also help muscles to relax more easily into sleep.

BEDTIME SNACK

Another part of the bedtime ritual for many families includes a bedtime snack. For optimal sleep, your child's snack should include a bit of protein and carbohydrate, possibly including milk or other tryptophan-rich foods, which encourage melatonin production. An example of a good bedtime snack might be a bit of cottage cheese or Greek yogurt and some canned, fresh, or dried apricots, or a slice of turkey on a piece of bread with a glass of milk or a cup of herbal tea. Avoid cocoa at bedtime; most contain too much sugar and caffeine, and may prevent your child from naturally drifting off to sleep.

CREATURE COMFORTS

Help your child let go of the day's anxieties by creating a calm and nurturing environment for sleep. Research indicates that people sleep better when a room is slightly cool (about 60–65°F; slightly warmer for babies) and when their bed is supportive, but comfortable. Smaller children do especially well with cozy blankets, and may feel more secure if their stuffed animals or "loveys" are with them in the bed. Use nightlights in your child's room if he is afraid of the dark, and provide additional nightlights in the bathroom and near your room so that your child feels secure once everyone goes to bed.

MANAGING INSOMNIA

Insomnia is usually seen as a nighttime problem, involving trouble falling or staying asleep. However, insomnia causes daytime problems as well, such as tiredness, lack of energy, difficulty concentrating, and irritability. If your child is not sleeping well, he may feel out of step with the world around him. Prolonged sleeplessness can cause health troubles, depression, and can even increase the potential for accidents and injury. Interestingly, the experience of insomnia has as much to do with one's perception of not sleeping well as with the actual amount of sleep. It will be important for your child to recognize that he may have a belief that sleep is difficult for him. Use a "letting go of the day ritual" so your child can associate its effects with sleep.

GET UP EARLY

One of the simplest ways to reduce anxiety is to get up earlier. Moving up your "start time" will help your body to be more ready for "quitting time" when the day is done. Depending on your child's age, you can adjust the time he gets up by fifteen to thirty minutes each day, and see how he responds after a week or so. Remember to factor in the amount of sleep your child needs according to his age when balancing bedtimes and rising times. An additional bonus of awakening earlier is that the extra time can be used for exercise or yoga, meditation, organization, and ensuring a good breakfast.

INCREASE ACTIVITY

Regular exercise boosts serotonin, making melatonin more available. It also tires and relaxes muscles, provides an outlet for stress, regulates blood sugar, and supports other bodily processes important to sleep. Keep exercise fun; try biking, rollerblading, or basketball. Some experts feel that morning activity boosts mood the best. If your child has insomnia, make sure he has some time to be active each day, as long as it's not too close to bedtime.

WHITE NOISE

Adding ambient sound such as a fan, water fountain, or white noise machine can help your child turn down the volume on anxious thoughts and create an external reference point which helps him to drop off to sleep. There are inexpensive sound machines available at many drug or department stores that can be set to any number of natural or created sounds. MP3s or CDs with ocean waves, crickets, or running water can also be helpful. If you are working on decreasing bedwetting, you may want to avoid water sounds, which might subconsciously affect your child's urge to urinate.

Important Points to Consider

Anxiety brings with it negative talk, self-doubt, and unhealthy coping behaviors. You need to help your child find positive self-love strategies so she can deal with her anxiety in healthy ways. Here are some things to keep in mind:

O Make sure your child is eating a balanced and healthy diet. Too much sugar and processed foods can have negative effects on the body and mind, which in turn can exacerbate anxiety.

O Talk to your child's doctor about the use of vitamins or herbs in her diet. Some of these have been found to help curb anxious feelings, but you'll need a doctor's help in selecting the proper ones for your child.

O Exercise is a proven good-mood booster. Get out and enjoy some form of exercise with your child. Make it fun and a daily occurrence.

O Proper sleep is pivotal for your child. Lack of sleep or poor sleep can increase your child's anxiety and her ability to self-regulate her emotions. Make sure your child gets enough sleep and create a positive sleep environment for her.

CHAPTER 13

The Case for Natural Healing: Alternative Therapies

If you find that traditional therapies only help relieve your child's anxiety to a certain degree and you feel more could be done for your child, it might be time to try some alternative natural therapies. Natural healing therapies have been used for centuries to restore and renew the body's internal systems. They can be used on their own or in conjunction with traditional medicine. An added bonus for some of these therapies is that through their experiences, children begin to value and learn about their own body's abilities. Taking your child to a professional who specializes in these therapies supports you as a parent, as you no longer have to be the only one educating and reinforcing these approaches.

Massage

Traditional healthcare systems are recognizing the therapeutic effects of massage in the healing process. Massage can restore the soul, rejuvenate the body, and decrease stress, and it's now a nationally certified healthcare option. Employers, doctors, chiropractors, even hospitals recommend and offer massage for wellness as a viable and beneficial therapy.

The type of touch used on a baby or child differs from that used on an adult. Massage for a child is more gentle and tender, and the length will be determined by your child's age and sensitivity to stimulation. When choosing a massage therapist, make sure the practitioner is certified and has expertise working with children.

It's also important to avoid sensitive or injured areas, to refrain from massaging a child who is ill or has a fever, and to avoid the stomach area for at least twenty minutes after your child eats. Keep in mind that massage can be done in a chair or strictly on your child's hands and feet. It is good practice to always ask your child permission before placing your hands on her.

BENEFITS

Massage has been found to decrease anxiety and slow down the heart rate. It can also increase attachment and bonding in the parent-child relationship when it is the parent who is giving the massage. Because massage can help children feel a sense of letting go, warmth, and care, your child's experience with massage may help her be more open to therapy. It may increase her ability to discuss issues related to why she feels anxious and increase the ability to trust in the helping profession. Physical advantages of massage include lowered blood pressure, slowed breathing rate, increased sense of comfort, improved circulation, and enhanced digestive functioning.

Hugs can be like medicine. It is believed that touch reduces anxiety because it promotes the growth of myelin. Myelin is the insulating material around nerves that makes nerve impulses travel faster.

WHAT THE RESEARCH SHOWS

In separate studies at the Touch Research Institute at the University of Miami School of Medicine, adolescents who received two chair massages over a month's time had decreased aggression, and those with ADHD had reduced anxiety levels, improved behavior, and rated themselves as happier. Massage therapy reduced anxiety and depression in children who were diagnosed with post-traumatic stress disorder after Hurricane Andrew in 1992. Infants whose parents gave them a massage before they went to bed slept better throughout the night and fell asleep more peaceably. Because massage stimulates all of an infant's or child's body, studies show it stabilizes heart rate and respiration, and increases the ability to cope with stress. Researchers also found that the level of cortisol, a stress-related hormone, decreased after a massage. Other research has shown that massage releases oxytocin in both the giver and receiver. The release of this hormone creates a "warm and fuzzy" feeling and may in part explain why bonding is strengthened during massage.

Chinese pediatric massage is also called Tui Na. It is said to influence a child's energy flow, much like acupuncture. The difference is that Tui Na uses gentle massage to activate energy meridians or blockages instead of needles. Treatment can start at birth, and is quick and effective until age six. After age six, regular acupressure can be used. In most cases treatment only takes one to two sessions for symptoms to abate.

HOW TO FIND A MASSAGE THERAPIST

To find a massage therapist, check out websites such as the American Massage Therapy Association (AMTA) at *www.amta.massage.org*, or The International Association of Infant Massage (IAIM) at *www.iaim.net*, which is a nonprofit national directory of certified infant massage instructors. They can help you find a massage therapist in your area, help you make decisions about what to look for in a massage therapist, and connect you with journals and research. Local breastfeeding centers may offer infant massage, and if you have a massage therapy training school in your area you may be able to receive chair massage for half the price. IAIM suggests you ask potential massage therapists a few questions, such as, is the therapist is certified or licensed, how much training she has done with children, and what the treatment method will be.

Acupuncture

The ancient system of acupuncture was developed over 3,000 years ago in China, and over the years has become recognized as an effective healing agent by Western health professionals. Today, acupuncture involves the use of fine needles placed in carefully chosen points, or meridians, once the practitioner has identified the disharmony within a person's body and mind. Most people associate needles with the pain of injections or having blood drawn. The needles used in acupuncture have no resemblance to those needles, however; they are much finer, solid instead of hollow, and tiny. Treatment can be one or two sessions or take a few months, depending on the target condition. As with all treatment options discussed, make sure your child is treated by a licensed acupuncturist (LAc). If your child is fearful about the process, you will likely be able to hold your child on your lap as he is being treated.

Traditional Chinese medicine includes herbs, and many acupuncturists may include herbs as a part of your child's treatment. Although the needling techniques have resulted in very few negative side effects, some herbs have been connected to more serious and frequent side effects.

BENEFITS

The Chinese believe that there is an energy flow called "qi" (pronounced *chee*) running throughout the body, and that acupuncture restores the balance of this energy flow, therefore eliminating symptoms of a disorder. With children and teenagers, acupuncture seems to be helpful in reducing anxiety, attention deficit disorder, addictions such as smoking, alcohol, food, or drugs, arthritis, asthma, circulatory problems, depression, general aches and pains, menstrual problems, sciatica, and skin conditions.

SHONISHIN

Shonishin originated in Japan in the seventeenth century. It is literally translated as "children's acupuncture" or "acupuncture for children." It differs from standard acupuncture because the practitioner does not pierce the skin, but instead uses an assortment of metal implements to gently stimulate the meridians and acupuncture points to move qi. This form of acupuncture, as with the standard kind, moves energy to unblock and strengthen the qi where it is weak, restoring balance in the child's body and a sense of calm. It is most useful for children from infancy through age five, although older children up to age twelve can benefit from this technique.

Aromatherapy

The use of essential oils and aromatic plants to affect mood or health dates back thousands of years to cultures including China, India, and Egypt and in fact receives several mentions in the Bible.

Two men are primarily responsible for bringing the use of flower and oil essences into the twentieth century. French chemist René-Maurice Gattefossé, who coined the term "aromatherapy" in the 1920s, was convinced that essential oils had antiseptic properties and began working with them in his laboratory. Edward Bach, who was a medical doctor and homeopathic physician in London, left a lucrative practice and went on to develop the Bach flower remedies.

While not aromatherapy, the Bach flower essences are another form of vibrational healing. By the time Dr. Edward Bach died in 1936, he had developed thirty-eight wildflower remedies. He created most of these remedies by testing them on himself first.

HOW AROMATHERAPY WORKS

Essential oils can enhance the mood, alleviate fatigue, reduce anxiety, and promote relaxation. It is believed that when inhaled, the essence works on the brain and nervous system through stimulation of the olfactory nerves. When a child breathes in the scent of an essential oil, electrochemical messages are sent to the emotion center of the brain, the limbic system. The limbic system then triggers memory and emotional responses, which send messages to the brain and body. If the oil is a calming one, like lavender or vanilla, aromatherapy can trigger the parasympathetic nervous system, which is responsible for relaxation.

Because children's skin and systems are delicate and sensitive, you must be very careful when using essential oils with them. It is also important to research an essential oil company ahead of time to make sure the oil is organic and does not have added chemicals. Although some practitioners feel that essential oils are not recommended for use on children at all, some believe that children over the age of six can use a short list of oil blends that are one-third to one-half as potent as what is recommended for adults.

Peppermint oil is useful for nausea and upset stomachs. To use, place two or three drops on a tissue, handkerchief, or natural cotton ball and hold it about 6 inches away from your child's nose. Be sure not to put it right under his nose; the smell might be too strong. Avoid getting the oil on the skin.

Lavender, chamomile, and mandarin are generally considered safe for children. Chamomile and lavender both calm anxiety. Chamomile has the added bonus of soothing digestion and is great with babies who struggle with colic. Lavender has a dual effect: It not only helps alleviate anxiety, it also lifts the spirits and is great for easing insomnia. In addition, lavender is known to have antiseptic properties and may help with headaches.

You can also massage your child with commercially prepared lotions, or use diluted oils in his bath. Be careful to use only essential oils; synthetic blends can cause allergic reactions and are unlikely to provide the same benefits as the original source. Also, be sure to carefully research the recommended percentage dilution of essential oils in carrier oil.

One of the best ways to bring aromatherapy into your home is through a diffuser. That allows the smell to diffuse slowly into the air. The Young Living company is a great resource for purchasing essential oils as well as diffusers.

You should also be aware that many "carrier oils" with which the essential oil is blended for dilution are nut-based, such as almond, macadamia, or hazelnut. So be aware that if your child has a nut allergy, these should be avoided. Nut-free oil alternatives include olive, sunflower, grapeseed, and avocado. It is best not to use aromatherapy on babies. Always consult with an expert, and never try to blend a potion on your own.

Biofeedback

Biofeedback evolved out of laboratory research in the 1940s to become one of the earliest known behavioral medicine treatments. The word *biofeedback* comes from *bio*, which means life, and *feedback*, which means "returning to the source." Years later biofeedback is commonly practiced by physicians, nurses, psychologists, physical therapists, dentists, and other professionals in private and hospital settings to treat adults and children with anxiety, and to address chronic physical conditions like pain.

HOW BIOFEEDBACK WORKS

Biofeedback is a painless, noninvasive technique that monitors the body's functions such as muscle tension, blood pressure, or heart rate, and "feeds back" the information to the patient. During a biofeedback session, your child will sit in front of a computer monitor with sensors on his skin that will measure one or more bodily functions. This will happen as he looks at animated games, cartoons, or stories, or listens to tones or melodies. The images and sounds on the screen change as your child learns to change his physical state and the associated feelings.

As he becomes more relaxed, opening up a channel of communication between himself and his body, he learns to regulate his anxiety and stress. The doctor or therapist will monitor the results on a separate screen, and give you and your child feedback on how he is progressing. Biofeedback can be an excellent self-help discipline, with each session lasting between thirty to sixty minutes.

Deepak Chopra, MD, and Dean Ornish, MD, created a software program called *The Journey to Wild Divine*, a biofeedback "game." Children can use this game at home to help learn about deep breathing and guided imagery in order to reduce anxiety.

EEG BIOFEEDBACK

EEG biofeedback, also referred to as neurobiofeedback, uses an electroencephalograph (EEG). This is a device that detects, monitors, and records the electrical activity in the brain, called brainwaves. Through the biofeedback machine, your child will learn how to increase or decrease brainwave levels. In general, the focus is on slowing brain waves to foster greater focus and calm attention. The most typical application for this technique is in treating ADHD, and it has also been found useful in treating anxiety and addiction.

WHAT BIOFEEDBACK CAN HELP

Biofeedback treatments can help a variety of medical concerns in children such as headaches, panic disorder, asthma, abdominal pain, sleep disorder, ADHD, stress, and addictions. As you can see, many of the conditions for which biofeedback is helpful also have anxiety as a component.

Biofeedback has two lines of benefit; on one hand, it can help your child become calmer and alleviate anxiety, chronic pain, insomnia, or muscle spasms. On the other hand, it can help your child become more alert, focused, and energetic, improving attention, concentration, school-work, or athletic performance. Biofeedback can enhance creativity as well as mental flexibility and emotional resilience.

Energy Work

You may not realize it, but you probably already use energy therapy every day. Think about it—your child can't sleep, so you go into her room, sit down next to her, and gently talk to her while rubbing her back—that's energy therapy. Or your child falls off his bike and you go to him, hold him in your arms, kiss his hurt knee, and hug him until the tears are gone—that's energy therapy, too. In each of those instances, you have passed your calm, loving energy to your child. That is also why you are the first person your child wants when she is hurt, you are the one she gives the harshest attitudes to, and you are the one she calls when she is scared. Your energy is what your children are seeking. It is unconditional, safe, and gives them comfort and strength.

WHAT IS IT AND HOW CAN IT HELP?

Energy therapy is a healing process that creates environments, philoso-phies, and therapies to support children who hurt inside. Much like acupunc-ture, it is done by correcting the imbalances in their internal energy. Most of the techniques are easy to learn and can be self-administered. Some examples of practices involving the use of energy to heal include the following:

- **Reiki and Johrei** are Japanese techniques for stress reduction and relaxation that many believe can promote healing. These are based on the idea that an unseen "life force energy" flows through all people and if it is low, then you are more susceptible to feeling anxious or getting sick, and if it is high, you can attain a sense of well-being.

- **Qigong** is based on the Chinese principle of "qi" energy. It is believed that different breathing patterns, when accompanied by certain motions and postures of the body, can enhance and create a sense of balance and calm, and release emotional and physical blocks. A tremendous amount of positive research is being released about the practice of Qigong and how it is being used in cancer therapy.

○ **Healing touch** occurs when a therapist identifies imbalances in your child's body and then corrects the energy. To accomplish this, the practitioner passes his hands over your child, without actually touching her.

○ **Prayer.** Praying for the healing of another or praying for love and support has proven to have many benefits to both the person stating the prayer as well as the receiver of it.

○ **EFT (energy field therapy) or TFT (through field therapy)** occurs when certain meridians on the body are touched to release an emotional or physical problem. EFT and TFT can be done anywhere, can be self-administered, are portable and efficient ways to calm the mind, and give a person a greater sense of control over anxious or distressing feelings.

Energy healing is a process that requires you to look beyond a symptom of illness, like the fact that your child is afraid to leave your side after a trauma, and instead look into your child's inner being to quiet her mind. The intent is to release the fear that created a blockage so your child can feel free again.

Blocks in energy are viewed as an attempt by the body and spirit to protect itself. Once your child stores the trauma or fear, she internalizes it, takes on the negative energy associated with it, and establishes a "new normal" so she can go on with life. Energy therapy can be used alone, or as a complement to any traditional or holistic treatment methods. Many believe it can reduce stress and anxiety, increase energy, improve physical health and wellness, and help your child feel more content.

Important Points to Consider

Oftentimes standard therapies may not work for your child and you may be left searching for other avenues to help your child's anxiety issues.

Explore some of these alternative therapies if you think your child may benefit from them:

O Massage can be a wonderful way to both soothe your child and connect with him. The process of massage helps you bond with your child while also helping him to relax and curb his anxiety.

O Sometimes just redirecting your child's energy can help him feel calmer. Simple acts such as soothing back rubs can help remove your child's energy blocks.

O The sense of smell has incredible influence on the body. Using techniques such as aromatherapy can help your child feel grounded and serene, which will help curb anxiety's hold on him.

O If your child seems unable to self-regulate his emotions and anxiety, it might be beneficial to look into biofeedback. Biofeedback helps open up a channel of communication between your child and his body, helping him see and understand his anxiety.

 **CHAPTER 14**

If It's Not Anxiety, Then What?

It can be frustrating to know be told that your child has a certain condition, but to know in your gut that there could be more. Because anxiety can be subtle and pervasive, it can either mimic or overlap with other conditions. It can also be brought upon by normal childhood characteristics, changes, and transitions. It is important therefore to be knowledgeable about the myriad other conditions that can mask anxiety or coexist with it. You will benefit your child by being informed about these other conditions in case she has questions for you regarding what is happening to her. It's not uncommon for other conditions such as the ones in this chapter to become less pronounced and therefore less of a struggle when strategies for relieving stress and anxiety are applied.

Overlap with ADD

Attention deficit disorder (ADD) is a neurobiological condition that interferes with a child's ability to focus attention, stay organized, resist impulses, and follow through on tasks. Dr. Daniel G. Amen, author of *Healing ADD*, identifies seven types of ADD, one of which he calls Anxious ADD. In *Healing ADD* he describes Anxious ADD as "inattentive, easily distracted, disorganized, anxious, tense, nervous, predicts the worst, gets anxious with timed tasks, social anxiety and often has physical stress symptoms such as headaches and gastrointestinal symptoms." His book provides solid research with SPECT imaging (brain imaging) evidence that supports a range of treatments, including visualization, hypnosis, supplements, and affirmations.

A child with ADD may feel an internal sense that the world is moving too fast, and he may have trouble paying attention because his mind is wrapped up in his multiple thoughts and worries. Children with anxiety can also suffer from thoughts and worries that seem unstoppable, and they may appear inattentive as a result. Similarly, children with ADD may experience depression or anxiety because it is so difficult for them to meet the demands of their world.

Because ADD can seriously affect your child's ability to learn, socialize, and develop the confidence, organization, and self-management skills he will need in adulthood, it is especially important to address this factor. Self-awareness practices (meditation, exercise, and guided imagery) can improve emotional and social functioning as they train your child to be more aware of himself and the world around him.

ACADEMIC CONCERNS

Most children with ADD show signs of their distractibility and/or impulsivity in the school setting. They may be unable to stay at their desks, focus on the teacher, or work for more than a few minutes without needing redirection. This applies to doing homework as well. It is typical for students with ADD to have trouble managing assignments, and completing and turning in homework. You or someone close to your child may see this as laziness or underachievement, but it is not. Children with ADD have physiological differences that prevent them from focusing. The overall effect is often reflected in poor grades or failure to progress in subjects. Children with anxiety often show restlessness and inattention as well, and may have trouble with homework if they feel overwhelmed.

Your child's teacher can usually tell you whether she suspects that ADD, rather than anxiety, is at the root of your child's trouble with schoolwork, or is an issue in the classroom. Keep in mind that ADD, because it lacks the behavioral component of hyperactivity, can be difficult to detect and may be more likely to mimic anxiety.

Children with ADD can benefit from energy techniques. Here's something you can try: Have your child stand up and march in place slapping opposite knee with opposite hand (for thirty seconds daily). This is a technique developed by author Donna Eden (*The Little Energy Medicine Book*) that increases the activity between the right and left hemispheres of your child's brain. Very often children with ADD have parts of their brain that are overactive while other parts are underactive. This exercise increases neuro-activity. One hemisphere is not better than the other, the idea is to get them working together to optimize your child's abilities.

BEHAVIOR CONCERNS

Children with ADD or anxiety may have behavioral concerns at home or school because of high levels of frustration. Typically, children with both disorders have more trouble transitioning between activities. For a child with anxiety, tantrums or meltdowns are often caused by fear, anticipation of failure, or feelings of being out of control. A child with ADD might exhibit problem behaviors because it is difficult for him to organize and sequence his thoughts and actions. Finding a tutor, ADD coach, or teacher who can teach basic organization skills can make a world of difference.

SOCIAL PROBLEMS

Children with ADD can have trouble making and keeping friends because of their impulsivity, which others see as odd or immature. Children with anxiety can also have unusual habits or ways of relating to others that can seem puzzling or unacceptable to their peers, as shared previously. For children who struggle with either, the rejection they feel can cause low self-esteem or depression, which leads to a sense of isolation and hopelessness about the future.

If your child's anxiety has obsessive qualities, he might spend hours writing one paper and not be able to complete any other work. This can look like laziness or procrastination to you. However, it is important to realize that, in this instance, your child's anxiety is driven by a need for perfection and the fear that whatever he does is never good enough and must be redone. Teach your child the value of making mistakes. Thomas Edison made 9,000 attempts when he invented the light bulb. When he was later interviewed by a young reporter, he stated, "I now know 9,000 ways a light bulb does not work."

TEMPERAMENT

Temperament consists of your child's inborn characteristics, such as shy, active, slow to adapt, adapt easily, sensitive to stimulation, etc. Most children have several traits that represent their temperament, not just one. It is important to note that these characteristics have been with your child since birth and most often can only be reported by a parent or caregiver. Children with sensitivity to their environment (e.g., stimulation, sounds, texture), who are slow to adjust, or who tire easily may be more susceptible to symptoms of anxiety. The earlier you recognize and accept your child's temperament style for what it is, the easier it will be to provide your child with tools that support his growth. It is the parents who want their child to change that may find themselves challenged by the symptoms. Temperament is not a life sentence, meaning that with compassion and tools such as the ones in this book your child can and will learn how to work with his traits in a way that serves him well.

Overlap with Depression

Depression is a mood disorder that can cause your child to feel tired, sad, lonely, bored, hopeless, or unmotivated for an extended period of time. In order for a clinical diagnosis in children, a depressive episode must last longer than two weeks and must interfere with daily functioning and/or be a change that is observable by others. Some researchers view anxiety and depression as two sides of the same coin. This is in part because both conditions involve disruption to the same neurotransmitters in the brain. In addition, symptoms of depression and anxiety overlap and may imitate each other. For example, many people with anxiety experience periods of depressed mood or other depressive symptoms such as guilt and feelings of worthlessness. Conversely, those with depression can experience states of agitation and worry that are very similar to the symptoms of anxiety.

THE IRRITABILITY FACTOR

Because children and adolescents aren't always capable of identifying and communicating their feelings and internal experiences to others, they are more likely than adults to show irritability when they are depressed. Irritable children and teens can be very difficult to be around as they never seem content, and may be negative or argumentative. Irritability is often contagious, and may snowball into conflict if it is persistent or extreme.

FEELINGS OF GUILT

Persistent feelings of worthlessness or excessive and unwarranted guilt can be very intense in both children and adults who are depressed. Guilt is also a strong component of anxiety, particularly if a child is old enough to feel she does not measure up to the expectations of peers, parents, and teachers. To help your child through these darker, heavier emotions, it will be important for you to model and teach her how to feel her emotions. Children and adolescents tend to focus on their primary feelings like sadness, anger, and happiness. Help your child to explore the range and variety of her emotions by getting her outside, connecting to nature, and disengaging from the busyness of life. Teach her to notice how grief sits heavy on the shoulders, and guilt is expressed through dropping our heads. By noticing her body's response, she is experiencing the physical manifestation and feeling of the emotion.

As your child sheds old belief systems ("I have anxiety") and emotions like shame, she opens the doorway to increasingly higher emotions, such as peace, love, and joy. As a result your child will feel more aligned with who she is, rather than what she is not.

PHYSICAL CONSIDERATIONS

When depression and anxiety are more serious, they can affect your child's ability to sleep and eat regularly. Children suffering from depression can experience loss of appetite, marked weight loss, or failure to make expected weight gains, while children with anxiety may also have trouble with their appetite and weight loss. Insomnia involving both the ability to fall and stay asleep can occur in both anxiety and depression, as can a diminished ability to think clearly, concentrate, and make decisions. Children with anxiety are more likely to show agitation, while depressed children are more likely to experience fatigue and lethargy.

SUBSTANCE ABUSE

People with depression and anxiety are at risk for developing alcohol or drug abuse. The use of chemicals to alleviate emotional distress is referred to as "self-medication." Teens with anxiety may be especially vulnerable, particularly if they use alcohol or drugs as a "social lubricant." Talk frankly with your children about your values and expectations regarding chemical use, and be alert for sudden changes in sleep, eating, energy level, and choice of friends, as these can all be indicators of chemical abuse.

Adjustment Disorders

It is common for children to experience changes in behavior and emotional upheaval when the world around them changes suddenly, as in a divorce or change of schools. In a child with anxiety, these challenges can be especially difficult because both his inner and outer world feel out of control at the same time. Both children and adults can experience adjustment disorders, and they are among the most commonly diagnosed mental health issues. In an adjustment disorder, there is a specifically identifiable stressor, which must have occurred no more than three months before the onset of emotional or behavioral symptoms. Adjustment disorders are generally short-lived, resolving in about six months after the original stress occurred. An adjustment disorder can involve depression, anxiety, or both. Behavioral disturbances can be common, especially in children who are more likely to "show" their feelings through their behaviors. Common events that might cause a child to experience an adjustment disorder are outlined next. If you are concerned that your child is having more trouble adjusting to change than he should, use the tips provided to help him cope, so that his anxiety does not become problematic.

MOVES
Moving to a new home is stressful for all families, and can be especially troubling if a child has to leave good friends or change schools. These transitions can be especially difficult in the middle-school years, when kids are working so hard to define who they will be and choosing a solid base of peers. For children with underlying anxiety, a move can be highly traumatic. If your child has anxiety, do your best to give him all the information you can and familiarize him with the new neighborhood. If the move is not long-distance, maybe you can take a walk through the new neighborhood, especially when a school bus is picking up or dropping off other children, or drive around and visit a nearby park and restaurants. After the

move, be sure to take the time to go back and visit old friends. Above all, let your child know that moving is not easy and listen to his fears. Validate the losses he will experience, and find ways he can be included in the familial team to make it a success.

ILLNESS OR DEATH IN THE FAMILY

Both sudden and chronic illnesses are highly stressful for families, and of course, the loss of a loved one is among the most stressful events a person can experience. When family life becomes upset or unbalanced, this can be very destabilizing for a child with anxiety. Children who spend excessive amounts of time away from their parents, because of lengthy hospitalizations for either themselves or a family member, can develop symptoms of anxiety and have more difficulty with developmental transitions.

Illness and death are mysterious and scary, especially for younger children. Experts say that it is best to give your child whatever information is available, but in a form that fits his level of development. There are many great books and other resources that can help younger children grasp serious life events at a level they can understand. Medical providers, places of worship, friends, and family are also great resources and support, and can buffer both you and your child from the anxiety inherent in managing illness and death.

BIRTH OF A SIBLING

Though the birth of a sibling is a new beginning for all families, it can be an especially difficult time for older children, particularly if they are already anxious. They now have to share Mom and Dad's attention, and they can sometimes feel alone and isolated when the rest of the world pays too much attention to the new baby. Children with anxiety may show increased trouble with separation, or regress (lose skills) in managing their emotions and behavior. Helpful tips include making sure you continue to spend one-on-one time with your child, and include him as much as you can in the new daily routines you are establishing. Consider giving your older child a special mother or father's helper job that includes him in the daily tasks. Avoid making older children responsible for the care of their younger siblings on a regular basis, as this can cause resentment and tension between the siblings.

BLENDED FAMILIES

Divorce, separation, and remarriage are events that naturally create a wealth of feelings for children, including anxiety. Sometimes even positive changes, such as a parent marrying a person the child really likes, can cause stress. General fears of the unknown, or uncertainty of where a child "fits" in the new family, are often undercurrents in children with anxiety. Blended families need time to adjust; be patient and remember to give your children special attention. Blended families who respect each other's backgrounds and outside family members, meaning they avoid negative, reactive comments or gossip, tend to adjust best. There are multiple resources on the Internet, at bookstores, through places of worship, or through community education to assist blended families.

Developmental Transitions

Your child is consistently learning, growing, and changing. This is hard work, and sometimes children can become snagged at particular stages in their development. The following sections detail some especially difficult times for children. Look back to the section on adjustment disorders for reference if you feel your child has more trouble in a particular area than most children her age. If your child does not seem to adjust well after four weeks, you may need to focus on strategies geared toward decreasing anxiety.

PRESCHOOL AND DAYCARE

Beginning school or attending a new daycare can cause anxiety in even the most well-adjusted children. Certainly, dropping a child off at daycare for the first time can be one of a parent's most difficult days. To ease transition, try to check in with your child each day after you pick her up, and send some small comfort items along with her, depending on your child's age. Examples might be a picture of you and your child together, a pocket-sized toy, a stuffed animal, or a favorite blanket. Be sure to keep in regular contact with your child's teacher and/or daycare provider to track your child's adjustment and discuss any concerns either of you may have. Generally, if your child appears happy when you pick her up at the end of the day and is excited to return the next, you can be assured that she is doing well in the new setting. Keep your goodbyes short and confident. For example, "I'll pick you up at the end of the day after reading time. Have fun!" Prolonged goodbyes tend to increase anxiety. Trust your gut and speak to your child's pediatrician and/or a parent educator if your concerns continue. Pay attention to your own levels of anxiety; if you are anxious dropping your child off, she will pick up on that. Stay calm, focused, and reassuring.

KINDERGARTEN

The transition to kindergarten can be full of anticipation and nervousness for both you and your child. The "official" school experience represents more time away from home, larger groups of kids, busing, and more adults to tell them where to be and what to do. Children with separation anxiety can be especially vulnerable at this time. Try to keep your routine the same at home, and talk to your child regularly to support and encourage her. It may be helpful to check in with your child's teacher or offer to help in the classroom if your child is struggling with separation. When you part from your child, keep goodbyes short and sweet. Consider a goodbye ritual, such as the way you kiss, hug, or give a high-five. The book *The Kissing Hand* by Audrey Penn is a wonderful book to read to children who are looking for ways to stay connected when they are not with you. Expose your child to the playground or building ahead of time.

MIDDLE-SCHOOL TRANSITION

Many children transition to larger schools with other unfamiliar children during middle school, and the demands for responsibility and self-motivation increase academically. Middle school is one of the most challenging times in a child's life, especially since she is likely to be experiencing hormonal changes at the same time. These physical and emotional changes contribute to the frustration and emotional pain she may be experiencing. Most of this is normal, but try not to minimize your child's interests in (and struggles with) friends, choice of leisure pursuits, dress, or music. Many anxious children at this age benefit from a mentor, older sibling, or therapist with whom they can entrust their trials and tribulations. Keep connected by inquiring about your child's interests, hugs, smiles, and through active listening or sitting in receptive silence. Hormonal shifts are often coupled with huge growth spurts, and create a need for a healthy diet, exercise, and lots of rest. It is normal for your adolescent to move away from things she was previously interested in. Try not to take your adolescent's behaviors personally. Take breaks to restore and replenish your patience.

HIGH SCHOOL

As your child moves into the high school years, pay attention to the times she appears resistant, critical, lazy, or unmotivated. Sometimes these are subtle signs of an underlying anxiety signaling that your child may be feeling the enormity of the pressures and responsibilities on her plate. During these times, your child needs to feel as if you are there for her through thick and thin. This doesn't mean that you won't expect your child to complete her responsibilities; rather, you will respond to her differently.

For example, instead of assuming she is lazy, treat her as if she is temporarily off balance. Consider connecting through open communication such as, "You seem off. Is everything okay?" You can also encourage your child to get back on task in a more compassionate way rather than through sharp demands and critical observations. Remember, setting boundaries and limits with your teenager is an act of love. Discipline helps children feel safe, yet allows them to test the waters without being left to experience severe consequence.

Shyness and Introversion

Introversion and shyness are temperament characteristics. Sometimes it is difficult to determine whether a child is shy, introverted, or truly has anxiety. Consistent avoidance of activities or chances to meet new people may signal that you need to look into your observations more carefully to rule out debilitating shyness or underlying anxiety.

WHAT IS SHYNESS?

Shyness is a term often used to describe those who avoid contact with others. A shy person may want to be social, but may experience physical symptoms of anxiety, which makes interaction with others uncomfortable. Shyness is actually a personality trait, and it can have many positive qualities. People who are shy often make good listeners who are sensitive, empathic, and are easy to be around. To sort this out, watch your child or teen in social settings and see if he is able to make eye contact and listen politely. If he seems happy with himself, and others feel comfortable around him, he may simply be introverted. In most cases, when provided with tools and social opportunities children learn to overcome their outward shyness. They may always feel a bit of inward shyness, but through tools and techniques learn to adapt and grow from it.

WHAT IS INTROVERSION?

Introversion is closely related to shyness, but introverts do not generally feel physically uncomfortable in social situations. Instead, introverts simply prefer to spend time in solitary pursuits, and "recharge" by spending time alone. Like those who are shy, introverts are often highly observant and introspective. It is typical for adolescents to appear quite introverted at times, as they may spend hours in their rooms gaming, grooming, or connecting with friends. Many gifted children can be introverted because their drive for learning and creativity pulls them inward. If you suspect your child's introversion is related to anxiety about social or other demands, this trait may need further exploration.

WHAT IS EXTROVERSION?

An extrovert is a person who delights in being in large groups of people and recharges by connecting with others rather than being alone. Extroverts can sometimes appear to be the life of the party, but they can also simply need a higher level of social contact than their more introverted peers. Even extroverted children who appear confident and savvy on the outside can develop anxiety. If your child has frequent meltdowns after social gatherings, or if you suspect he is a "great actor," anxiety may be something to look further into.

The Overextended Child

Professionals and parents today are concerned that their children are over-extended. Though researchers agree that some structured activity is good for kids, the goal is to balance structured time with free time. If your child has anxiety, you'll want to be especially sensitive to how she seems to handle the demands of her schedule to help her from becoming overwhelmed. Conversely, some children with anxiety have trouble with unstructured time because they have difficulty making choices and initiating activity. As such, you may need to coach your child a bit on how to create structure for herself. The tips that follow will help you determine if your child is overscheduled.

SIGNS YOUR CHILD IS OVEREXTENDED

Signs that your child might be overprogrammed include frequent fatigue, resistance, or refusal to attend activities, complaints about or lack of enjoyment of activities, aches and pains, frequent irritability, persistent feeling that there is not enough time, frequent illnesses, and worry. If your child regularly experiences more than one or two of the things on that list, it may be time to have a sincere talk with her about how to cut back on activities. Allowing your child to make her own choice about what she would like to let go of is an act of self-love.

SIGNS YOU MAY BE OVEREXTENDED

If you as a parent are overextended, you may experience any of the things on that list, too. Some additional questions to ask yourself include: Do I feel like I spend my life in the car, going from one activity to the next? Do I skip meals or eat them while driving? Do we have time to be together as a family? Do I create time for hobbies and leisure? Am I getting enough sleep? Depending on your answers to these questions, it might be time to consider reducing the amount of activity you and your child are involved in. Sometimes eliminating even one obligation can reduce stress dramatically and help everyone to breathe a bit easier.

Separation Anxiety

A young child who is scared of new people and places is normal. However, if a child has continued intense fear that something is going to happen to someone he loves and he stops normal activities, this could be a sign of a larger issue. Separation anxiety disorder affects about 4 percent of children ages six through twelve, and research shows treatment is often successful.

FACTORS TO CONSIDER

Environmental and temperamental factors that seem to characterize children who suffer from separation anxiety disorder are an extremely close-knit family, a fearful or extremely shy temperament as an infant, shyness or passivity in girls aged three to five years old, or an insecure parent who found it difficult to attach in infancy.

THE DEVELOPMENTAL PROCESS

When your baby was born, you might have noticed he easily adapted to new surroundings and people, which is typical of babies six months old or younger. Actually, with infants, it is usually the parents who have more anxiety than the child when being left with a babysitter or in a new environment! A peak in separation anxiety is expected between the ages of eight months and one year, although some children experience it later, between eighteen months and two and a half years old, and some may never experience it at all. During this time, you may find you cannot leave the room for even a moment without your child becoming agitated and upset.

Consider speaking to your pediatrician, who will most likely ask you questions about your child's school experience. As always, trust your gut. If you feel the present situation may not be a good match for your child's needs, you may need to seek another program. Some children thrive in a smaller, less stimulating environment, while others do better where there is more movement. Parents discover a great deal about their child's learning styles in these early years.

> Separation anxiety can be considered developmentally normal up until around age six. Many times, such as in a preschooler, it is a sign of healthy attachments to loved ones, an example being a five-year-old that clutches your leg for several minutes before you leave. However, if the distress continues beyond your child's same-aged peers, and increases in duration, frequency, and intensity, you will want to seek help from a professional.

Stranger anxiety is also something to be aware of during early childhood. It is evidenced when your child clings onto you for dear life, his huge, panicky eyes looking like you are going to feed him to a dinosaur if you even try to give him to another person. As time goes by and your child learns to feel safe and secure in the knowledge that you really are going to return, and he really will be given back to you, the anxiety usually fades. It is if he continues to experience excessive fear that seems out of proportion at the start of his elementary school years that you will want to seek support from a qualified professional.

Important Points to Consider

Many other conditions can have anxiety as a symptom or cause. You may have thought your child had only anxiety issues only to discover it was only the tip of the iceberg. In addition, some events can trigger anxiety. Whether the change is a new school, new living conditions, or the loss of a loved one, be understanding of your child's unique needs. Change can be difficult for all children but especially for those with anxiety.

Here are some things to consider:

O Prepare your child for change as much as possible. If she is changing to a new school, let her visit the new school well in advance of the change. If the change is a new home, allow her to be part of the home selection process and listen to her opinions.

O Knowing how to support your child through change in order to make successful transitions is critical. It is especially important in considering major childhood "life event" changes, such as attending a new school, moving, divorce, or a death in the family.

O For unforeseen or sudden changes such as death, be open and honest with your child. She may have unsettling questions, but this is often how children with anxiety deal with change—by amassing as much knowledge about the situations as they can. Answer your child as truthfully as possible and resist the urge to sugarcoat things.

O Help your child find avenues to express her feelings about the change. Drawing, journaling, or talking with a trusted person could all be methods to help your child.

Choosing Therapy

If your child has symptoms of anxiety, you will want to first schedule an appointment with your family doctor. Because the symptoms of many physical illnesses are closely related to the symptoms of anxiety, you want a clean bill of physical health. Once that has been established, your doctor may suggest a referral to a therapist, but you can also do your own research to seek out a qualified therapist or practitioner. Whoever you choose, make sure the professional is licensed and comes highly recommended. In addition to a therapist, you may want to work with other practitioners, like energy practitioners, nutritionists, coaches, or other specialists.

Individual, Family, and Group Therapy

In general, there are three types of therapy: individual, family, and group, and many of the therapies described in the following sections can be used in all three settings with a child with anxiety.

INDIVIDUAL THERAPY

Individual, one-to-one, or talk therapy, is the most common psychological therapy for children and adults. Individual therapy is based on the premise that when a trusting relationship with a therapist is established, a client can increase self-awareness and change destructive or unhealthy patterns of thought, emotion, and behavior. A real-life example is when you feel relief from and resolution to an issue by talking it through with a supportive friend. Though theoretical approaches vary, most individual therapy is based on the concepts outlined as follows. However, it is important to keep in mind that some schools of thought, such as behaviorism, focus almost exclusively on behavior change and bypass the importance of the therapeutic relationship and the need for emotional catharsis, or release.

"Name It, Claim It, and Tame It"

In a broad sense, "name it, claim it, and tame it" captures the essence of personal growth, both in therapy and in life. The ability to identify a problem or pattern such as anxiety, take ownership of the problem, and take steps to change it are at the root of personal development. Individual therapy is designed to facilitate this process while offering support, suggestions, affirmation, and a compassionate ear.

Positive Psychology

Individual therapy usually begins with an assessment of what's not working for a client with respect to thinking, emotions, relationships, and behavior. A skilled therapist will help clients identify maladaptive or unhelpful patterns, and set measurable goals to decrease them while increasing more positive, productive patterns. Because of the inherent negativity in anxiety, a therapist who helps your child own and build on her strengths can be essential.

For younger children, the use of play, art, or other child-centered techniques will almost always be incorporated into the session, and for adolescents, who are more verbal and reflective, talk therapy is more common. Many therapists incorporate mind and body practices such as breathing, meditation, and EFT into their sessions.

Creating Change

The crux of any successful therapy is the ability to which it is effective in creating lasting change. Usually, therapy continues until the changes are stable; that is, new patterns of thinking, acting, feeling, and interacting are used more often than not to meet life's challenges. Careful observation and goal setting at the beginning of therapy are crucial to being able to assess the extent to which a child has been successful in changing old, less functional patterns. It is exciting to see how each change your child is able to make creates opportunities for more learning and growth to occur.

FAMILY THERAPY

Family therapy grew out of individual therapy as psychologists began to realize that family patterns, interactions, and wounds contribute to both the problem and the solution to emotional and behavioral troubles. There are several schools of thought that drive family therapy, but the overall premise is that families exist as systems, and that "the whole is greater than the sum of its parts." With younger children, parenting and/or family therapy may be preferred, as parents and siblings have the most direct impact on a child's world. Other components, such as individual play therapy or skill building, can be added to your child's plan of care based on her needs.

Family Dynamics

Family dynamics is a term used to describe the general pattern and functioning of your family. Family therapists look at patterns of communication, alliances, problem solving, and the assignment of power and resources, among other things, to determine a family's overall style and then assess what about that style is working and what is not. Family therapists also assess a family's adjustment to various transitions, coping, parenting styles, and marital stability to determine which areas might need to be addressed.

Extended Family

Extended family, such as grandparents, aunts, and uncles may be included in family therapy for a number of reasons. This can be especially important if extended family members provide care for your child or if the contact is especially close, so that your child's new skills and the techniques she is learning are supported and reinforced in as many settings as possible. If you have a strong relationship with your family already and feel they can be team players, you will more than likely be able to enlist their support for your child without the assistance of a therapist.

Parent Coaching

Parent coaching can be offered individually or in groups, and is often woven into individual therapy when a therapist provides focused time for parents without the child present. Parent coaching can be an essential tool in helping parents to ally with each other, and help their children by reducing anxiety created by mixed messages or approaches. Some therapists integrate parent coaching into their sessions while others may be more hands-off. If you are not receiving parent coaching consider seeking additional services and or classes.

GROUP THERAPY

Group therapy can be a powerful tool for decreasing isolation, increasing confidence, and practicing emotional expression and social skills. One of the primary benefits of group therapy occurs when a child realizes that she is not alone in her fears and struggles, and that she is not as different from others as she may have come to believe.

Behavioral Groups

Behavioral therapy in the group setting is designed to help people learn new skills and let go of old, ineffective ones. Training and practice in social skills and assertiveness can be especially helpful for children with social phobia, and teaching relaxation and other coping strategies can be done effectively in a group setting. The group itself allows for trial and error, direct feedback, support, and opportunities for immediate reinforcement of new skills.

Although true for most children, teens and tweens can especially benefit from group therapy. This is because of their strong need to connect with, and be accepted by, peers. Groups are also excellent ways to help kids reduce feelings of isolation and alienation. This concept in itself can go a long way to reduce anxiety.

Parenting Groups

Parenting groups that provide opportunities for both peer support and skills training are available in many communities. Though many parenting groups are based on childrearing and discipline, there may be specialty groups in your area that are suited to your particular needs. Well-run groups understand the power of unity and connection.

Supportive Approaches

Supportive therapy is a general term to describe any number of interventions that are intended to reduce discomfort and enhance the effectiveness of therapy for your child. Supportive therapy can be used together with individual, family, or group therapy, and may be recommended by your mental health provider if she feels it will be helpful for you and your child. Several types of supportive therapy are highlighted here.

COORDINATION WITH OTHER PROVIDERS

It is sometimes essential for a care provider to coordinate with others who support your child. For example, therapists often consult closely with pediatricians or psychiatrists to help monitor a child's response to medication. If your child shows school avoidance or refusal, contact with his teachers and other school staff can ensure that his transition back to school is the smoothest it can be.

PEER COUNSELING

Peer counseling is intended to help your child build trust, gain support and confidence, and decrease isolation through his connection to a peer counselor. Peer counseling may be available at your child's school, either in groups or one-to-one, and community resources may offer similar opportunities for you or your extended family.

MENTORS

A mentor is an older, more experienced person who can take you or your child under his wing for support and education. Good mentors for children with anxiety might be older students, siblings, or family members who have tackled anxiety issues, or school personnel who have had similar experiences. Make sure that you know and trust your child's mentor so that your own anxiety will not complicate your child's opportunity to benefit from the relationship.

ANIMAL COMPANIONS

Pets can be wonderfully supportive: They ask for little, are great listeners, and generally do not talk back. Companion animals and their therapeutic benefits have become more popular over the past decade, and there have even been specific "animal therapies" developed for special populations.

Research shows that sitting with and stroking a cat or dog reduces muscle tension and blood pressure, and slows breathing and heart rate. As such, a child who may feel challenged learning relaxation techniques may benefit just as much by sitting quietly with her pet.

To enhance your child's ability to achieve relaxation while connecting with a pet, you can encourage him to slow down, speak softly (or not at all), and breathe deeply. Finally, the responsibility of caring for a pet is a great way for an anxious or worried child to develop confidence and mastery.

Play Therapy

Play therapy is a projective technique in which your child's conflicts and desires are revealed through her play and her interaction with the therapist. Generally, play therapy is the mode of choice for children under the age of ten to twelve, as they are less verbal and abstract than older children. As children mature, their ability to "think about thinking" and work with their emotions directly increases, and play techniques give way to more traditional talk therapies, which focus directly on emotional expression, problem solving, and behavioral change. It is important to note that play that occurs in a professional setting is different from play that occurs outside of the office. Unless your child's therapist guides you, it is generally unwise to attempt to make free play "therapeutic."

THE SYMBOLIC NATURE OF PLAY

Play therapists work from the assumption that the symbols your child uses in her creative play are windows into the deeper recesses of her fears, desires, and motivations. When she expresses these through her play, they gradually become a part of her awareness; that is, she can learn about herself when guided by someone who is observant and responsive to her non-verbal messages. When your child feels fully understood, she is more likely to trust that she can manage her emotions and solve her problems.

THE CATHARTIC NATURE OF PLAY

When your child expresses her inner nature through her play, a natural emotional release called catharsis occurs. This emotional response can also uncover other, related emotions. For example, a girl who re-enacts a fight with her father in play therapy may feel relief, or might move from anger to sadness as her role in the conflict becomes clearer. Your child can then use her insights to change her self-talk and behavior about the situation, and make future adjustments. When an anxious child expresses fears or worries in therapy, they lose some of their power to torment her in her daily life.

> The practice of "acting as if" can encourage a child with anxiety to try out new ways of thinking and acting, which may bring relief from fear, worry, or withdrawal, and lead to new ways of acting outside the therapy office. Storytelling and role-playing are also techniques that draw on "make believe."

LEARNING NEW BEHAVIOR THROUGH PLAY

Play therapists are trained to gently comment on and intervene in play to help your child learn new behavior. For example, in the situation just described, a therapist might model a father and daughter having a talk together or making up, or suggest that a child come up with a different, more satisfactory scenario. In addition, though much of play therapy itself is unstructured, there are multiple opportunities to teach social skills such as developing confidence, taking turns, following the rules of a game, and negotiating. Play therapists incorporate all of these skills to help a child with anxiety develop confidence, decrease his need for control, and tolerate anxiety.

Art and Music Therapy

The creative arts are a perfect medium for the expression of personal experiences, emotions, desires, and aspirations. Therapists skilled in these areas may use a variety of techniques to identify and address problem areas for a child. Opportunities for creative expression also allow children to build on strengths and increase confidence.

MUSIC THERAPY

Music therapy is commonly offered in a group setting, such as residential treatment, and is relatively uncommon in general practice. Music can be a great vehicle for eliciting and expressing emotion, such as fear or sadness. In fact, if you were to watch a movie without the music track, you might find the drama of the story far less compelling. A music therapist can play particular music to draw on certain emotions that your child can explore more fully. Conversely, a music therapist may suggest your child use various musical instruments to express a particular feeling or problem.

ART THERAPY

Art therapy can use any medium to help your child explore and express his experiences and emotions. Drawing, as you have seen, can be a useful tool in both assessment and therapy. The use of paint, clay, chalk, and collage materials is also common in art therapy.

DO YOU NEED A SPECIALIST?

In many areas of the country, it may be hard to find specialized art and music therapy. However, therapists may incorporate art or music into sessions with your child, depending on their skill and interest. It is worth mentioning that building confidence through art, music, or performance can be extremely helpful for children with anxiety. However, if a child shows high levels of performance anxiety, this type of therapy may be too overwhelming and may not be appropriate.

Cognitive-Behavioral Therapy

Cognitive-behavioral therapy (CBT) is probably the most widely researched of all types of therapy. It was developed in the 1970s as behavioral psychology began to push the field toward more specificity, effectiveness, and measurability. Cognitive therapy focuses primarily on how to change destructive thought patterns; behavioral therapy helps people identify and change unhelpful behaviors, and replace them with new, more effective skills. Put the two together and you get CBT. CBT is offered in both group and individual therapy, and may be used as a component of family therapy as well. Cognitive therapy is useful for tweens and teens who are developing the ability to monitor and change their thinking, and behavioral therapy can be especially helpful for younger children who need their world to be manipulated more directly.

THOUGHTS RULE

The term "cognitive" refers to the thought processes, both positive and negative, which in turn drive our emotions and behavior. Cognitive statements include messages you give yourself about events in your life, messages you have internalized from and about your past, and messages about your future success or failure. The goal of cognitive therapy is to minimize negative, self-defeating thoughts, and to maximize positive, supportive, and growth-oriented thoughts. As you can see, cognitive therapy is one of the most crucial components of treatment for anxiety, no matter what the age of the client may be.

SKILLS TRAINING

Simply titled, skills training is used to help people learn new patterns of behavior and to replace older, less effective patterns. Skills training is crucial for children with anxiety so that they can gradually build small skill sets (like calling friends) in order to develop larger skill sets (like going on a sleepover). Skills training can be used along with behavioral management to increase the impact of practicing the new behavior. Other uses of skills training for children with anxiety include teaching a shy child how to ask for help, or helping a teen learn how to be more confident by building social skills.

ASSERTIVENESS AS ANTIDOTE

Assertiveness has been well researched as an antidote to anxiety, and has been popular in both group and individual therapy for decades. Though many people feel anxious when they anticipate having to assert themselves, the act of self-assertion actually decreases anxiety by producing a sense of mastery and control over the environment. Even small children can benefit from assertiveness training at very basic levels, by learning to identify and express their feelings and to ask for help if they are worried or uncomfortable. This is particularly crucial for a child with anxiety, who may feel so overwhelmed by emotion that she can't soothe herself or garner support.

BEHAVIORAL MANAGEMENT

Though behavioral management is not always viewed as an aspect of CBT, it is a useful tool in helping children with anxiety. A typical use of behavioral management in therapy is for you, your child, and her therapist to develop a systematic plan to reinforce, or reward, her progress. For example, if a child who has been school-avoidant attends school for a full week, you might reward her with a special treat, outing, meal, or quality time together.

When to Consider Medication

Placing your child on medication does not mean you have failed; it is simply a choice you and your child are making at this point in your child's journey. However, if you start your child on medication without implementing additional tools, strategies, and supports his journey may not evolve in the way you had hoped. Anxiety is an opportunity to increase your child's awareness and abilities to move through stress-related experiences and emotions. Some pediatricians or psychiatrists are quicker to put children and teens on medication than others. If something does not feel right, trust your gut and consider getting a second opinion. Sometimes someone in the same office, such as a nurse practitioner, can help you make an informed decision. If you do choose to use medication as part of your child's treatment, make sure that he takes it consistently and at the same time every day. Medication can sometimes increase anxiety, so you should also discuss a weaning strategy with your doctor if it becomes necessary for your child to stop taking a particular medication.

Important Points to Consider

The type of therapy you choose should be a family decision, one that incorporates your child's opinion as well as your own. Some children might feel more comfortable in a group setting and others might tend toward a more individual approach. You know your child best, and by being open and communicating with your child, you can find the best avenue for her.

Here are some other points to keep in mind:

O Therapy has been proven to be of great benefit for children with anxiety. In fact, when your child expresses her worries in therapy, they lose some of the power over her in her daily life.

O Be ready to be there for your child if she wants to ask your opinion of, or wants you to be part of, her therapy. Conversely, do not take it to heart if your child does not want to share a lot of information with you. Remember that it is not about you, it is about your child.

O Anxiety is an opportunity for your child to navigate stress-related experience and emotions. If your child's doctor is too quick to put her on medications, you may need to look for a second opinion.

O Whatever type of therapy your child opts for, remember to keep an open mind and heart for whatever may come. Therapy can at times bring up uncomfortable feelings for your child or yourself, but by keeping connected and positive, you can more fully reap the benefits of the therapy.

**CHAPTER 16**

Creating a Promising Future

If you are raising a child with anxiety, you may be worried about your child's future. Questions like *Will my child grow out of this? Will she be able to live a healthy, happy life?* and *Will it ever be easier for her?* may often be on your mind. This is particularly true if it concerns your firstborn or only child. In your heart you may want to be hopeful for a promising future, but your mind tells you to be uncertain. This chapter offers you a glimpse of how children who may have experienced anxiety at one point in their lives look in the future.

What Is the Goal?

The long-term goal for assisting children with anxiety is twofold: First, for your child to feel confident that she is capable of handling just about anything that is presented in her life; and second, for her to recognize her own internal and external discomfort as an opportunity for growth. This means rather than being overwhelmed or pulled along by her feelings, she will embrace them as part of her wholeness. Your child's feelings and physiological responses are not the problem. It is how she chooses to perceive them and thus react that determines whether she will learn and thrive from anxiety.

Help your child develop an ally relationship with his emotions. Emotions have tremendous value, and give you and your child insight about the quality of energy in his body. When emotional energy is distorted, your child is more likely to base his responses on fear. When emotional energy runs fluidly, your child is able to recognize and choose a response from love.

LEARNING TO LET GO

Looking ahead to a promising future requires a bit of letting go on your part. As much as you may dread the future or your child growing up too fast, the reality is that he will be an adult someday, and adulthood comes with everyday stressors, challenges, and, in some cases, hardship. If you have an attachment to how you would like the outcome to be, or put pressure on yourself to do the right thing, you may actually contribute to a future of struggle.

The path of letting go requires you to acknowledge and experience your fearful thoughts. Parents who choose to ignore, disregard, or distract themselves from their own fearful thoughts may inadvertently project them onto their child. Projection comes in many forms, and even if you are not verbally expressing your fearful thoughts, your child can sense them. On the outside, you are juggling many things. On the inside, however, what gets sacrificed is the experience of allowing yourself to feel your emotions.

Part of letting go means making time for yourself, and tuning in to your senses through practices that connect you to feeling rather than doing. Take a moment and imagine a tightly wound ball of yarn. Now imagine gently loosening the yarn with your fingers while breathing in and out slowly. Letting go is similar, only instead of yarn, emotions such as fear have been tightly wound up. Consider the symptoms of anxiety, often experienced in the chest and head, to be a road map of where in your body you may be holding tension. It is as if your body is saying, "Here it is." Now relax and breathe, and you will soon see how you have the ability to convert this tension into release.

Attachment to outcomes creates anxiety. Be open and willing to allow your child's journey to unfold in its own way. Attempting to direct or change the outcome may interfere with her progress. Instead, release your own fears and trust that with love, support, and practice your child is already moving her symptoms of worry, tension and fear. Anxiety is not the problem, it is the non-movement of emotional energy which can lead to physical and emotional symptoms. Trust your child's body has the ability to release anything that is not serving her while taking in information (thoughts, experiences) and sensations that do. Be mindful of impulsive reactions such as jumping to conclusions (e.g., "This isn't working") or giving up on a support (strategy or service) before giving it adequate time. Having a support person you trust and feel confident in (e.g., therapist) is essential.

Surrender Expectations

Anxiety and expectations go hand in hand; therefore, if your child is experiencing symptoms of anxiety it is likely that expectations are in the mix—expectations of herself, school, siblings, and so on. You may also have expectations about what her life will be like. Learning how to recognize and surrender expectations allows you to understand and grow. The following steps will show you how:

1. Identify what expectations feel like. Some people can identify them by an urge or impulse to make things different. For example, you expect your child to clean up, and then immediately do it for her because it makes you feel too anxious to wait.

2. Ask yourself, "What am I expecting right now of myself and others?" For example, are you expecting things to be done quickly or without discomfort?

3. Once you identify your expectations, begin to disarm them. To do this, bring the expectation to the forefront of your mind and then imagine yourself pushing the disarm button on your keychain for your car. Take a couple of minutes, and one by one disarm two or three of the expectations you may be carrying.

The road to a promising future means keeping realistic expectations, which for some parents and children means accepting the fact that emotions are not designed to go away, but rather are a part of the way human beings connect, learn, and evolve.

See the Blessing

Whether you have modeled these strategies to your child or implemented them with her, there are most certainly blessings that you have experienced as a result. To help your child move toward a more promising future, it is important to periodically review the progress the two of you have made. Think of all the times you choose to take a breath and watch your words rather than react impulsively. Encourage your child to think of the things she has learned about herself, what worked and didn't work, and yet how each and every step (immediately successful or not) helped prepare her for where she is today. Reflect on what a gift it has been to walk alongside your child through this process. As your child moves toward adulthood, you will continue to walk with her, but instead of walking side by side, she will gain confidence and begin to lead the way.

NEW WEALTH

One of the goals of transitioning your child into adulthood is to help her recognize that she can handle anything that comes her way. In order to do this well, it is important for you and your child to value health as wealth, physically, mentally, and emotionally. If you feel good inside, this will be reflected on the outside. Explain to your child that she'll know when she is feeling good when she is able to make responsible decisions, see mistakes as opportunities for growth, and see problems as feedback and opportunities rather than obstacles.

> Encourage your child to take three slow breaths before beginning and ending his day. Tell him to imagine a clear bubble forming around him as he breathes. Breathing and visualizing in this way can help insulate his body from negative, toxic energy and environments.

In order to keep healthy in mind and body, you and your child will need to consistently create healthy boundaries between work, rest, exercise, and play. This will allow you to more easily recognize when you are overextended. (This often shows itself through forgetfulness, or making careless errors.) Self-love strategies are a part of how you live your life, rather than something you hope to try one day.

Trust Yourself

As you embark on the pathway to a promising future, you will find that trusting yourself comes more easily. As a parent, you know your child better than anyone else in the world. If you are able to see yourself clearly as well, you are in a great position to use your intuition and a bit of courage to know when to step back and hand your child the reins. This means that sometimes you may have to stand by as your child moves through discomfort, let him experience his own consequences, and manage your own anxiety all the while. You may also have to encourage other family members to do the same. Trust your instincts also if you truly feel that your child is overwhelmed by the strategies and other goals you've set together, or if the pace is moving too rapidly or too slowly. There will be times when your child takes the lead, as well as times when you will choose to take a step forward and get more involved.

LAUNCHING

Just as the job of a good therapist is to prepare a client to end therapy, your job as a parent is to make sure your children have the skills they need to become independent and to continue growing and learning from all the experiences in their lives. Your child's increasing independence can be scary, lonely, confusing, and sad. Sometimes it helps simply to reassure yourself that it's nature's plan for your child to leave the nest and continue to do your best to allow your child to soar.

As you learn to let go of your child, you can stay flexibly connected, securely but not too tightly. Be prepared to handle strong emotions as your child becomes less dependent upon you. This can be especially true when separation anxiety is an issue. It's always best to try not to let your own fears interfere with your child's desire and need to push forward. Draw on your inner and outer resources, and know that you and a million other parents have learned to let their children go on to be competent, productive, resilient, responsible adults.

PRACTICE MAKES PERMANENT

Scientists have known for years that learning involves physical changes in the brain. Eric R. Kandel, a neuropsychiatrist and winner of the 2000 Nobel Prize in Physiology or Medicine, proved that the release of neurotransmitters increases as learning occurs, creating new neural structures and connections, which multiply and further enhance learning. Learning interpersonal skills and social interaction is complex, requiring more repetition to acquire. This has applications to managing social anxiety, assertiveness, and learning when and how to seek support from others. Practices that relieve stress and anxiety are a lifetime commitment, and with that comes the reward of being able to access your higher potential at each state in your entire lifespan.

Also, keep in mind that your child is unlearning old, unhelpful behavior at the same time that he's learning new skills. According to Kandel, though it does not take long for the brain to store a new image or idea, new cell growth and connection does require quite a bit of repetition and reinforcement to truly take root. Your child will need to continue practicing new skills such as better self-talk and self-calming skills.

TAKING STOCK OF YOUR TOOLBOX

After a couple of months of implementing strategies and other possible interventions, it will be important to reflect on the progress you and your child have made in your work to overcome his anxiety. The questions that follow can help guide you.

These same questions may be used as a way to determine whether to discontinue other supports.

- Have you and your child learned what anxiety is, and how it is triggered?

- Have you addressed any medical, nutritional, or environmental concerns that contribute to your child's symptoms?

- Has your child improved in his ability to use his voice? Is he able to identify and express his needs and feelings effectively?

- Are you and other family members more able to share your needs and concerns without undue upset or conflict?

- Have you, as a parent, addressed your own expectations and fears?

- Does your child use skills such as breathing, relaxation, and imagery with minimal or no prompting from you?

- Can your child self-soothe in other ways, such as yawning, bathing, music, exercise, and breathing?

- Are release strategies a part of your daily lives? Does your child set an intention to release the thoughts, feelings, and beliefs that surface?

- Does your child view stress in a helpful or harmful way?

- Does your child know what an emotion is, and how to experience it without fighting or being overwhelmed by it?

- Does your child set healthy boundaries for technology and media?

- Does your child understand the difference between coping and releasing?

- Has your child experienced relief from the strategies you have implemented?

WEANING GRADUALLY

When your child hears about his growth and gains from people such as his teachers, family members, or therapist, this can be a great source of pride and accomplishment. As your child becomes more confident in his abilities and more self-assured, you may begin to decrease support. For example, if your child is receiving extra help from a tutor, or support from a school counselor or nutritionist, you may start scheduling more space between appointments.

When ending support services, keep in mind that your child (and you) may have developed a strong attachment to the individual providing them. Honor the effort and the relationship, and avoid ending abruptly, unless you have reason to believe it is harmful or inappropriate for your child to continue. To help with closure and acknowledge your child's accomplishments, consider planning something special for the final session, or ask about exchanging touchstones.

Moving on from Medication

Research shows that many people are able to manage their anxiety effectively after stopping medication, typically if they have received therapy to learn ways to work through their symptoms. Specific data on exactly how this applies to children with anxiety is less conclusive, due to the fact that children's development is dynamic and ongoing, along with the current lack of longitudinal research.

BASIC GUIDELINES

In general, it is common practice for a child to stay on a medication for at least six to twelve months in order to obtain maximum benefit. However, timeframes vary depending on the class of medication. For example, it is typical to see benefits from antidepressants in around four to six weeks. In addition, if it takes time to reach the therapeutic dose of the medicine, or if another medication is added, it may take longer to see optimal effects. Your child's age, the length and severity of her symptoms, and the co-occurrence of other mental health issues will also determine when it is reasonable to discontinue a medication.

> Your child may need to stay on medication through times of transition or particular stress, during anniversaries of loss or trauma, or during the fall and winter months if seasonal affective disorder is a concern. It may be unwise to risk further unbalancing your child when times are already difficult.

Though most medical professionals would agree that a child shouldn't take medication she no longer needs, there are just as many reasons to continue until full benefit can occur. Unfortunately, it can sometimes be difficult to determine just when to discontinue a medication, especially if it has been used for an extended period of time.

Letting Go

As you work through anxiety with your child, you've most likely learned to avoid letting your own fears and needs interfere with the well-being of you and your child. It can be challenging to continue to keep yourself in check as your child gets older and becomes more independent. Here are ways that you can promote independence as your child grows.

1. **Encourage independence.** In order for your child to have the confidence that he can manage on his own, he needs to feel that you

believe that he can do it. Always let your child make an attempt, no matter what his age, before you step in. This applies all the way from learning to walk to applying for college. If your child seems to have trouble managing on his own, offer support while respecting his growing independence by considering the tip that follows.

2. **Ask before offering.** If you see your child struggling, simply ask him if he needs feedback, assistance, or direction. If he does, help him make a plan by breaking down the problem and coming up with small steps. As your child becomes stronger and more independent, he may begin to decline your assistance; take this as a sign of growth and accomplishment, not as rejection. The best strategy is always to allow your child the time and space to figure things out on his own before you step in. This is especially important for young adult children who have moved out or gone away to college. Always be sure to lend a sympathetic ear, but use your reflective listening skills to guide and encourage, rather than dictate. Be careful in offering advice that is unsolicited.

When looking at colleges and other places to live, be sure to look into what is available on and off campus to support healthy living. Many colleges now offer yoga classes for college credit, free meditation groups, stress management courses, massage, healthy foods, counseling, gyms, healthy eating options, and housing that is less noisy than a dorm room.

3. **Have a plan.** As your child grows, it will be important for him to learn how to be aware of when normal stress develops into anxiety. Occasional anxiety is normal (e.g., finals week at school); however, teach your child to pay attention to the frequency, intensity, or duration of symptoms. Symptoms such as worry, perfectionism, panicking, or insomnia are signs that your child may need support or to make some changes. Comfort your child that symptoms are the body's way of communicating that it is out of balance. Some-

times a simple shift in schedule can ease the pressure, allowing your child to resume a balanced lifestyle. Other times, it may be a sign that your child needs a tune-up. Therefore, it is important that you maintain connections with professional and nonprofessional people that your child can go to during times of stress such as transition times, unemployment, holidays, breakup of a relationship, or a dip in grades.

MOVING OUT

Whether it is a new apartment, shared housing with friends, or the transition to college, your child may experience his first real sense of independence when he moves out of your home. For some, this can be exhilarating; for some, frightening; and for most, a combination of the two. To help your child manage separation and general anxiety, make a plan for how you'll stay connected, and acknowledge that this is a big change for both of you. Clarify guidelines for how often you will talk on the phone, and set limits if you feel either you or your child is too dependent on the contact.

If your child will be living nearby, you might consider starting a Sunday dinner ritual, a monthly night at the movies, or a Saturday coffee break. Young adults are often comforted by care packages, impromptu grocery deliveries, or occasional offers to help with housework. Remember, though, to ask before you offer, and respect your young adult's need for privacy and the right to establish a life of his own.

Ask your child if his anxiety could speak words, what would it say? Perhaps it would say, *Thank you for taking the time to notice the symptoms and for having the courage to speak up and attend to it, rather than ignore or shove it away.* It might say, *I never wanted to be fixed, but rather loved and treated with kindness and respect.* It may whisper *Good job, you have everything you need to be the best you can be.* It may reveal that this was all part of your child's personal story of how he learned to receive the moment, be himself, trust his higher guidance, and love himself.

Appendix:
Additional Resources

Bourne, Edmund J. *The Anxiety and Phobia Workbook, Third Edition.* (Oakland, CA: New Harbinger Publications, 2000).

Boyle, Sherianna. *The Four Gifts of Anxiety: Embrace the Power of Your Anxiety and Transform Your Life.* (Avon, MA: Adams Media, 2014).

Buell, Linda Manassee. *Panic and Anxiety Disorder: 121 Tips, Real-Life Advice, Resources and More.* (Poway, CA: Simply Life, 2001).

Burns, David D. *When Panic Attacks: The New, Drug-Free Anxiety Therapy That Can Change Your Life.* (New York, NY: Morgan Road Books, 2006).

Ellsas Chansky, Tamar. *Freeing Your Child from Anxiety.* (New York, NY: Broadway Books, 2004).

Dispenza, Joe. *Evolve Your Brain: The Science of Changing Your Mind and Breaking the Habit of Being Yourself.* The Aware Show interview. November 2013. *www.theawareshow.com.*

Flora, Carlin. "Challenging Success-via-Failure," *Psychology Today,* July/August, 2015.

Foa, Edna B., and Wasmer Andrews, Linda. *If Your Adolescent Has an Anxiety Disorder.* (New York, NY: Oxford University Press, 2006).

Fox, Bronwyn. *Power over Panic: Freedom from Panic/Anxiety Related Disorders, 2nd Edition.* (NSW, Australia: Pearson Education Australia, 2001).

Foxman, Paul. *The Worried Child: Recognizing Anxiety in Children and Helping Them Heal.* (Alameda, CA: Hunter House Publishers, 2004).

Gardner, James, and Bell, Arthur H. *Overcoming Anxiety, Panic, and Depression.* (Franklin Lakes, NJ: Career Press, 2000).

Lee, Jordan. *Coping with Anxiety and Panic Attacks.* (New York, NY: Rosen Publishing Group, Inc., 1997, 2000).

Lin, Helen Lee. "How Your Cell Phone Hurts Your Relationships," *Scientific American*, September 2012.

McGonigal, Kelly. *The Upside of Stress.* (New York, NY: Avery, 2015).

Nardo, Don. *Anxiety and Phobias.* (New York, NY: Chelsea House Publishers, 1992).

Wagner, Aureen Pinto. *Worried No More: Help and Hope for Anxious Children.* (Rochester, NY: Lighthouse Press, Inc., 2002).

Weintraub, Pamela. "The Voice of Reason," *Psychology Today,* May/June 2015.

Williams, Mark; Teasdale, John; Segal, Zindel; and Kabat-Zinn, Jon. *The Mindful Way Through Depression: Freeing Yourself from Chronic Unhappiness.* (New York, NY: Guildford Press, 2007).

Websites

NYU School of Medicine Child Study Center
Articles, research, programs, and education about children.
www.aboutourkids.org

American Academy of Child & Adolescent Psychiatry
Information about diagnosis and treatment of developmental, behavioral, and emotional disorders that affect children and adolescents.
www.aacap.org

American Academy of Family Physicians
www.aafp.org

American Medical Association
www.ama-assn.org/ama

American Psychological Association
Helps you find a psychologist in your area.
www.apa.org

Anxieties.com
Self-help site with tests, publications, and information.
www.anxieties.com

Anxiety and Depression Association of America (ADAA)
Comprehensive website about anxiety.
www.adaa.org

Common Sense Media
Use this website for advice on all types of media and technology.
www.commonsensemedia.org

Healthy Place
Offers information, live discussion, and chat groups.
www.healthyplace.com

Healthychildren.org
Includes guidance on family media, TV, and cell phones.
www.healthychildren.org

MentalHelp.Net
Resource for consumers and professionals.
www.mentalhelp.net

National Alliance on Mental Illness (NAMI)
General mental health resource includes opportunities for support and networking.
www.nami.org

National Institute of Mental Health (NIMH)
Up-to-date news, research, and treatment information about anxiety.
www.nimh.nih.gov/health/topics/anxiety-disorders/index.shtml

Psych Central
A mental health website that has created a social network run by mental health professionals.
www.psychcentral.com

Specialty Resources

Communication
Advocates for Youth website provides a good resource for multiple issues with children.
www.advocatesforyouth.org

This web page gives a list of feeling words to help you and your child learn ways to express emotions.
www.psychpage.com/learning/library/assess/feelings.html

Massage
Massage Magazine has articles of every kind about massage and studies about the health aspects of massage for children.
www.massagemag.com

Biofeedback
Association for Applied Psychophysiology and Biofeedback, with information about providers, research, and treatment.
www.aapb.org

Conscious Living Foundation has books, stress-management tools, CDs, and movies to guide children in relaxation techniques and understanding how the body works.
www.cliving.org/children.htm

Aromatherapy
Aromatherapy and Children article by Kathi Keville, Mindy Green (excerpted from *Aromatherapy: A Complete Guide to the Healing Art* found at the Health World website).
www.healthy.net/Health/Article/Aromatherapy_and_Children/1714

Chiropractic

The International Chiropractic Pediatric Association is a resource that provides an accumulation of research and a membership directory for the layperson interested in chiropractic care for his or her family.
www.icpa4kids.org

Resource to find studies and articles on chiropractic care for children.
www.chiro.org/pediatrics/ABSTRACTS/Chiropractic_For_Children.shtml

Homeopathic Medicine

The National Center for Homeopathy has created a website to provide access to studies, resources, and practitioners.
www.homeopathic.org

National Center for Complementary and Integrative Health is an excellent resource for alternative options.
http://nccam.nih.gov

Other Sites

The Self-Love Movement

This movement encourages people to sign up to commit to take care of themselves daily. Inspirational videos and quotes are shared on this site along with a free guidebook.
www.facebook.com/TheSelfLoveMovement

StressFreeKids

Books, CDs, curriculums, and other products designed to empower children, teens, and adults.
www.stressfreekids.com

The LifeSkills Program

An audio-recorded learning process designed for the anxious person aged six through fifteen. LifeSkills can be used by a professional therapist, classroom teacher, or monitored by a parent.
www.chaange.com/about-lifeskills

Young Living

A resource for purchasing essential organic oils.
www.youngliving.com

YouthBeat

An empowering website for youths aged six through eighteen.
www.youthbeat.com

InspireMeToday.com

Recommended for short inspirational daily readings.
http://InspireMeToday.com

Index

Acupuncture, 182–83
Adjustment disorders, 197–99
Alternative therapies
    acupuncture, 182–83
    aromatherapy, 183–85, 189
    biofeedback, 185–87, 189
    energy therapy, 187–89
    massage, 180–82, 189
    shonishin, 183
Anchors, importance of, 70–71, 129
Anticipatory anxiety, 63–66
Anxiety. *See also* Stress
    avoidance and, 49–50
    behavioral expressions, 48–49
    biological aspects of, 39–40
    causes of, 35–45
    "contagious" anxiety, 32–33
    coping strategies for, 23–24,
        76–77, 146–47, 157–62
    curbing, 164–65
    environmental factors, 42–45
    gender comparison of, 36–37
    genetic causes of, 40–41
    goal for, 220–23
    increasing, 166–68
    physical aspects of, 57–59
    prevalence of, 36
    psychological aspects of, 37–39
    releasing, 146–47, 162, 173–74
    signs of, 47–60
    similar conditions, 191–206
    symptoms of, 47–60
    therapy for, 179–89, 207–18
    understanding, 11–12, 21–33

Aromatherapy, 161, 183–85, 189
Art therapy, 214–15. *See also*
    Therapy
Attention deficit disorder (ADD),
    192–95
Avoidance behaviors, 49–50

Behavioral expressions, 48–49
Behaviors, understanding, 18–19,
    48–51
Biofeedback, 185–87, 189
Biological aspects, 39–40
Birthday candle exercise, 161
Body awareness, 94–95
Body pain, 58–59
Boundaries, 83–84
Brain, strengthening, 128–29
Brain, understanding, 39–40
Breathing techniques, 147–50, 162
Bullies, 70–71, 75, 84–85

Calming techniques, 157–62. *See
    also* Self-love strategies
Chanting technique, 158
Children
    boundaries for, 83–84
    coping strategies for, 23–24,
        76–77, 146–47, 157–62
    developmental transitions for,
        199–201, 206
    discipline for, 131–43
    extroverted children, 202–3

Children—*continued*
  giving full attention to, 17–19
  goal for helping, 220–23
  introverted children, 201–2
  overextended children, 203–4
  pressures on, 76–77, 203–4
  promising future for, 219–29
  resilient children, 141–43
  separation anxiety in, 204–5
  shy children, 201–2
  social concerns of, 75–88
  temperament of, 41, 44, 194–95,
    201–4
  thriving children, 103–6
  understanding anxiety, 21–33
  understanding emotions, 94–95,
    100
Chimes/bells, 158
Cognitive-behavioral therapy
  (CBT), 215–17. *See also* Therapy
Communication skills
  in home environment, 90–93
  "I" messages, 90–92, 100
  listening skills, 92–93, 228
  reframing language, 93,
    127–29
Community resources, 96
Conscious parenting. *See also*
  Parental concerns
  active approaches for, 118
  benefits of, 14–17
  consistency for, 116–18
  co-parenting, 98–99, 123–25
  for defusing situations, 121–22
  empowerment tools for, 125–27
  explanation of, 13–16
  follow-through for, 116–18
  intentional planning, 118–19
  overprotective parents and, 106–8
  parenting "dos," 138–39
  patience for, 119–21
  pointers for, 105–6, 115–29

positive reinforcement, 40,
    139–41
  proactive approaches for, 118
  reframing technique, 93, 127–29
  routines, 122–23
  rules and, 125–27
  strengthening right brain, 128–29
  tips for, 105–6, 115–29
Consequences, 132–38. *See also*
  Discipline
Consistency, importance of, 116–18,
  129
Co-parenting, 98–99, 123–25
Coping strategies, 23–24, 76–77,
  146–47, 157–62
Crystals, 66–68
Cyberbullying, 75, 84–85

Daycare concerns, 199–200
Depression, in children, 195–97
Depression, in parents, 108–9
Developmental transitions, 199–
  201, 206. *See also* Transitions
Diet concerns, 164, 166–68, 176–77.
  See also Nutrition
Discipline
  consequences, 132–38
  parenting "dos," 138–39
  positive reinforcement, 40, 139–41
  punishment, 137–38
  resilient children, 141–43
  rewards, 141–42
  self-control, 132–34
  self-regulation, 132–34
Doctors, 58, 82, 97, 107–8, 168–69.
  See also Therapists

Emotions, understanding, 94–95,
  100
Empathy, 16–17

Empowerment tools, 125–27
Energy medicine, 160–61
Energy, redirecting, 127, 133, 189
Energy therapy, 187–89
Environmental factors, 42–45
Exercise, 165, 171–72, 177
Extroversion, 202–3

Family. *See also* Parental concerns
    blended families, 111–13, 199
    death in, 198, 206
    divorce in, 111–13, 199
    illnesses in, 198
    siblings, 97–98, 198–99
    support from, 89–100
Family therapy, 209–10. *See also*
    Therapy
"Fear of fear," 63
Feelings, understanding, 94–95, 100
Follow-through, 116–18, 129
Food concerns, 164, 166–68, 176–
    77. *See also* Nutrition
Friendship challenges, 56–57, 60,
    69–70

Gender comparisons, 36–37
Genetic concerns, 40–41
Grounding techniques, 66, 146, 165
Group therapy, 210–11. *See also*
    Therapy
Guided imagery, 154–55

Healing techniques, 179–89. *See also*
    Alternative therapies
Healthy habits, 44–45, 165–72,
    176–77
Herbal supplements, 168–69
High-school concerns, 201. *See also*
    School concerns

Home environment
    communication in, 90–93
    connecting to truth, 96–98
    creating support team, 95–96
    parenting styles in, 99–100
    support from family, 89–100
Homeostasis, 57–58

"If only" thoughts, 26–29
Imagery, 154–55, 162
"I" messages, 90–92, 100
Individual therapy, 208–9. *See also*
    Therapy
Insomnia, 175
Intentional planning, 118–19
Introversion, 201–2
Isolation, 50–51, 60

Journaling, 174, 206

Kindergarten concerns, 200. *See also*
    School concerns

Letting go, 220–22, 226–29
Letting go ritual, 110, 173–75
Life events, 42–45, 197–201, 206.
    See also Transitions
Listening skills, 18, 69, 92–93

Mantras, 160
Marriage concerns, 98–99, 109–13,
    199
Massage, 180–82, 189
Mealtimes, 67–68, 79–80, 86, 164
Media guidelines, 75–83, 88
Media messages, 75–79
Medical support team, 96

Medication
  considering, 217, 218, 227
  monitoring, 212
  side effects of, 168
  stopping, 226–27
  substance abuse and, 196–97
  therapy and, 217, 218
Meditation techniques, 150–52, 162
Meltdowns, 48, 71, 122, 193, 203
Middle-school issues, 71, 200–201. *See also* School concerns
Mindfulness, 14–15, 22, 103, 128
Mindful transitions, 48–49, 69, 197–201, 206
Mineral supplements, 170
Mood-boosters, 164, 171, 177
Mood disorders, 195–97
Mudras, 159
Music therapy, 214–15. *See also* Therapy

Natural healing
  acupuncture, 182–83
  aromatherapy, 183–85, 189
  biofeedback, 185–87, 189
  energy therapy, 187–89
  massage, 180–82, 189
  shonishin, 183
Negative rehearsal, 64–66
Negativity, 26–30, 38–39, 157, 209
Nervous habits, 59
Neurotransmitters, 39
Nutrition, 44, 166–71, 176–77
Nutritional supplements, 168–70

Overextended children, 203–4
Overlapping conditions
  adjustment disorders, 197–99
  attention deficit disorder, 192–95

depression, 195–97
mood disorders, 195–97
Overprotective parents, 106–8

Parental behavior, 103–8
Parental concerns. *See also*
  Conscious parenting
  blended families and, 111–13, 199
  co-parenting, 98–99, 123–25
  depression and, 108–9
  letting go, 220–22, 226–29
  marriage concerns and, 98–99, 109–13, 199
  overprotective parents and, 106–8
  parental choices, 102–3
  parental influence, 43
  parental roles, 102
  parenting styles, 99–100
  school concerns, 61–73
  thriving parents and, 103–6
Parenting styles, 99–100
Patience, 119–21, 129
Peer pressure, 69–70
Perfectionism, 29–30, 38, 53, 228
Physicians, 58, 82, 97, 107–8, 168–69. *See also* Therapists
Play therapy, 213–14. *See also* Therapy
Positive reinforcement, 40, 139–41
Positive thinking, 26, 30, 45
Preschool years, 199–200
Pressures, 76–77, 203–4. *See also* Social concerns
Procrastination, 49–50, 54, 117, 120–21, 194
Progressive muscle relaxation (PMR), 152–53
Psychological concerns, 37–39

Reflective listening, 92–93, 228
Reframing technique, 93, 127–29
Reiki, 160
Relationship concerns, 98–99, 109–13, 199. *See also* Parental concerns
Relaxation techniques, 147–53, 157–62
Resilient children, 141–43
Resources, 231–34
Rewards, 141–42
Routines, importance of, 70–71, 122–23, 129
Rules, importance of, 125–27, 129

School concerns
    anxiety and, 51–56, 61–73
    bullies, 70–71
    gossip, 70–71
    high-school years, 201
    homework concerns, 53–56, 60, 62, 73
    kindergarten years, 200
    middle-school years, 71, 200–201
    negative rehearsal, 64–66
    parental involvement, 71–73
    peer pressure, 69–70
    preschool years, 199–200
    skipping school, 51–53
    staying involved with, 71–73
    test anxiety, 63–65
Self-awareness, 14–15, 29–30
Self-control, 14–15, 132–34
Self-help, 97, 124–25, 186
Self-love strategies
    breathing techniques, 147–50, 162
    exercise, 165, 171–72, 177
    guided imagery, 154–55, 162
    meditation techniques, 150–52, 162
    nutrition, 166–71, 176–77
    progressive muscle relaxation, 152–53
    relaxation techniques, 147–53, 157–62
    self-soothing strategies, 157–62
    self-talk techniques, 155
    sleep routines, 172–75, 177
    visualization techniques, 153–55
    worry warriors, 156–57
    yoga, 171–72
Self-reflection, 32–33
Self-regulation, 132–34
Self-soothing strategies, 157–62
Self-talk techniques, 155
Self-trust, 223–26
Separation anxiety, 204–5
Shonishin, 183
Shyness, 201–2
Siblings, 97–98, 198–99
Singing bowls, 158
Situations, defusing, 121–22
Sleep routines, 45, 172–75, 177
Social concerns
    boundaries, 83–84
    coping with, 76–77
    cyberbullying, 75, 84–85
    influences, 75–87
    media guidelines, 79–83, 88
    media messages, 75–79
    online predators, 84
    pressures and, 76–77
    social media, 82–88
    technology guidelines, 75–83, 88
Social media, 82–88
Social skills, 76–77, 86–88, 96–97, 210, 214–16
Spiritual resources, 96
Stranger anxiety, 205
Stress
    anxiety and, 22–23, 30–32
    benefits of, 22–24

Stress—*continued*
  releasing, 146–47, 162, 173–74
  worry and, 24–29, 156–57
Stressors, 38–39, 42–44, 173–74
Support
  communication and, 90–93
  for emotions, 94–95
  from family, 89–100
  at home, 89–100
  social support, 71
  support team, 95–96
Supportive therapy, 211–13. *See also*
  Therapy

Tantrums, 23, 122, 193
Tapping technique, 65–66, 73,
  158–59
Tearfulness, 48
Technology guidelines, 75–83, 88
Teenagers
  cognitive-behavioral therapy for,
    215–16
  consequences for, 137
  coping with pressures, 76–77
  fears of, 19
  group therapy for, 211
  medication for, 217
  negative rehearsal for, 65
  school concerns for, 56, 201
  self-soothing strategies for, 157
  substance abuse and, 196–97
Temperament, 41, 44, 194–95,
  201–4
Test anxiety, 63–65
Therapists, 97, 209–15
Therapy
  alternative therapies, 179–89
  art therapy, 214–15
  benefits of, 218
  choosing, 207–18

cognitive-behavioral therapy,
  215–17
family therapy, 209–10
group therapy, 210–11
individual therapy, 208–9
medication and, 217, 218
music therapy, 214–15
play therapy, 213–14
supportive therapy, 211–13
types of, 207–18
Touchstones, 66, 73
Transitions, 48–49, 69, 197–201, 206
Trauma, 43–45, 197–99, 206
Trust, 223–26
Truth, connecting to, 96–98
Truth statements, 155, 162

Validation, 17, 92, 142, 198
Video games, 78–81
Visualization techniques, 153–55
Vitamins, 169–70

"What if" thoughts, 25–26
Worry, 24–29
Worry warriors, 156–57
Worrywarts, 156–57

Yoga, 171–72